EASY PIANO

CHRISTMAS SONGS
IN EASY KEYS

"Christmas Songs in Easy Keys" include no more than one sharp or one flat in the **key signature**.
The key signature appears on the left side of every staff, right next to the clef signs.

no sharps or flats

one sharp: F#
all Fs are played as F#

one flat: B♭
all Bs are played as B♭

Sometimes **accidentals** appear. Accidentals are sharps and flats not in the key signature.
An accidental alters a specific note in a particular measure. The next bar line or a
natural sign (♮) cancels an accidental.

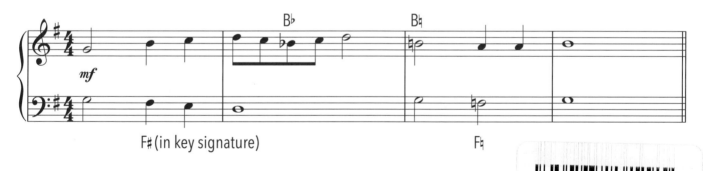

F#(in key signature)   F♮

ISBN 978-1-70514-164-9

T0057214

HAL•LEONARD®
7777 W. BLUEMOUND RD. P.O. BOX 13819 MILWAUKEE, WI 53213

Visit Hal Leonard Online at
www.halleonard.com

Contact us:
Hal Leonard
7777 West Bluemound Road
Milwaukee, WI 53213
Email: info@halleonard.com

In Europe, contact:
Hal Leonard Europe Limited
42 Wigmore Street
Marylebone, London, W1U 2RN
Email: info@halleonardeurope.com

In Australia, contact:
Hal Leonard Australia Pty. Ltd.
4 Lentara Court
Cheltenham, Victoria, 3192 Australia
Email: info@halleonard.com.au

BELIEVE
from Warner Bros. Pictures' THE POLAR EXPRESS

Words and Music by GLEN BALLARD
and ALAN SILVESTRI

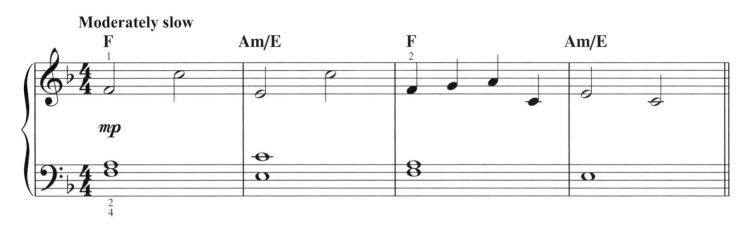

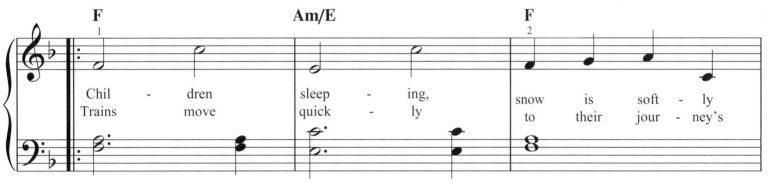

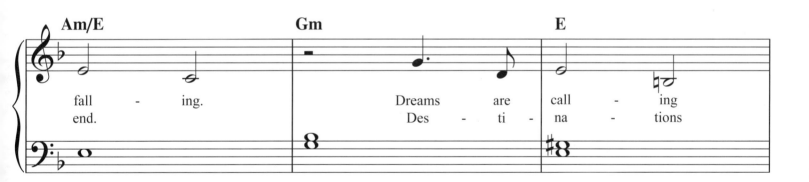

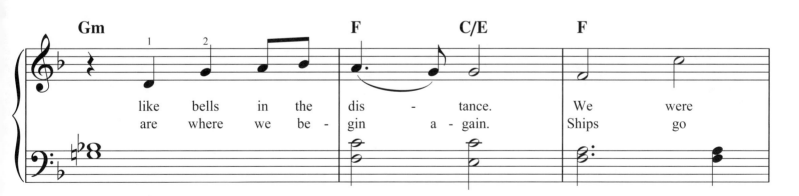

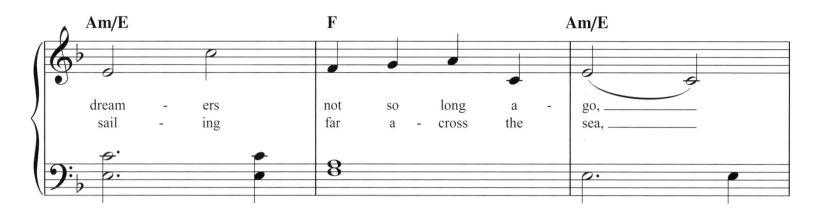

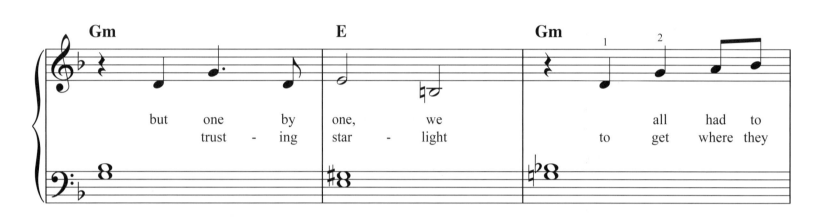

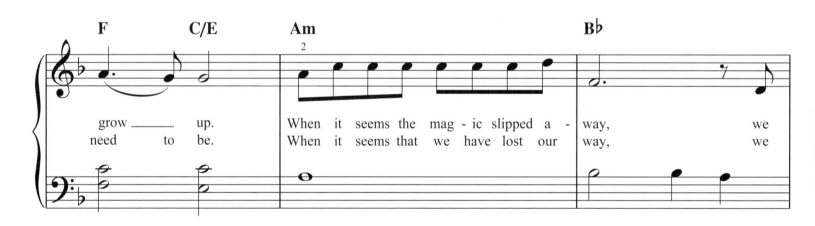

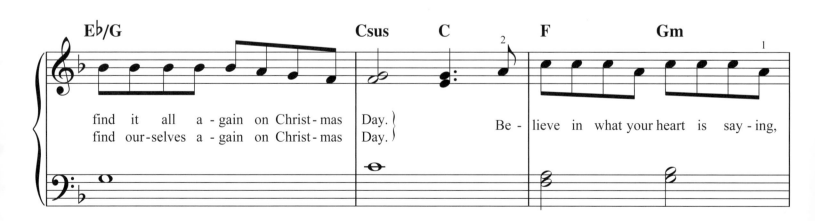

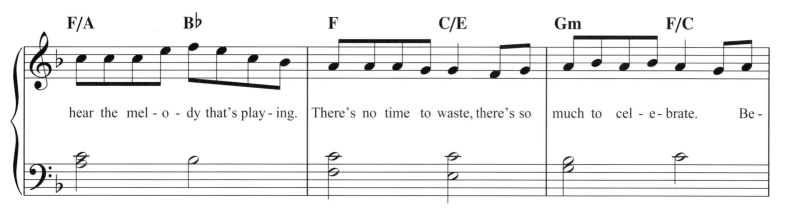

hear the mel - o - dy that's play - ing. There's no time to waste, there's so much to cel - e - brate. Be -

lieve in what you feel in - side and give your dreams the wings to fly.

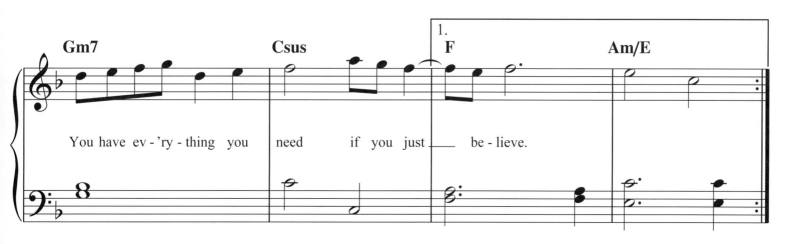

You have ev - 'ry - thing you need if you just ___ be - lieve.

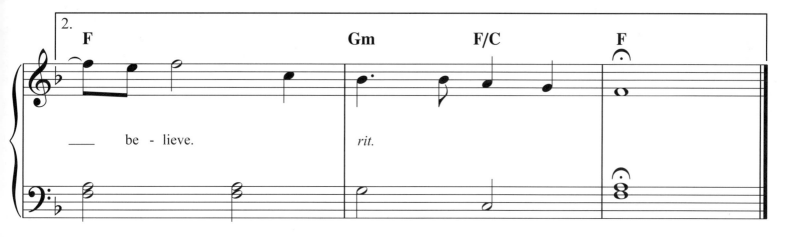

___ be - lieve. *rit.*

All I WANT FOR CHRISTMAS IS YOU

Words and Music by MARIAH CAREY
and WALTER AFANASIEFF

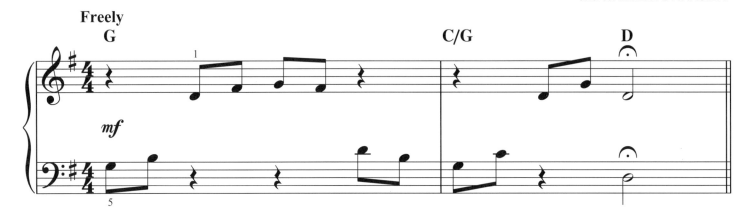

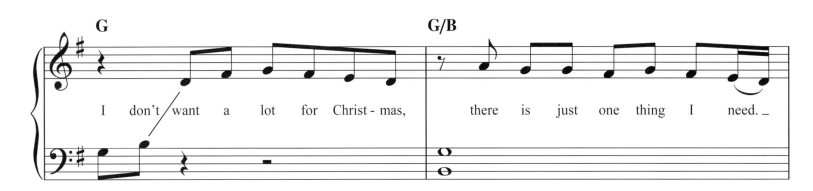

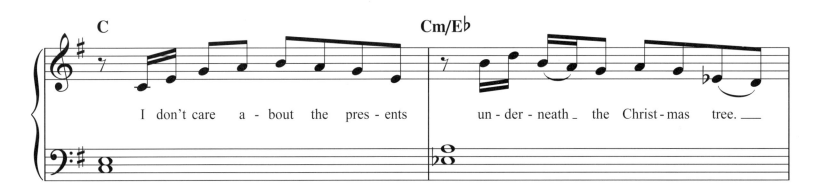

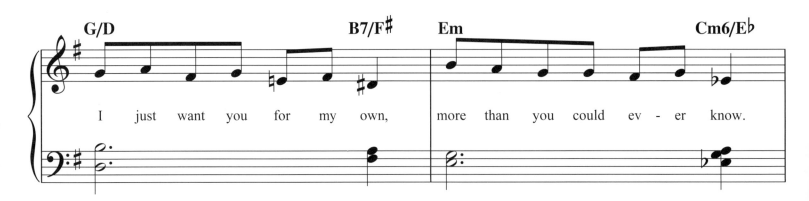

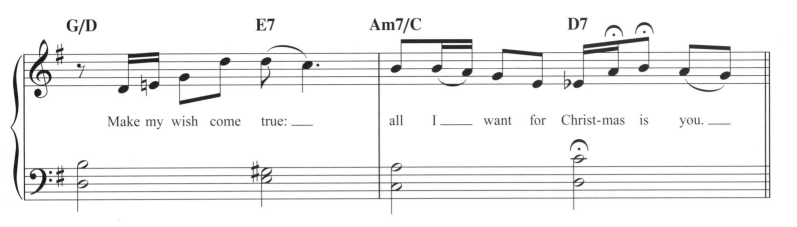

Make my wish come true: ____ all I ____ want for Christ-mas is you. ____

Moderately

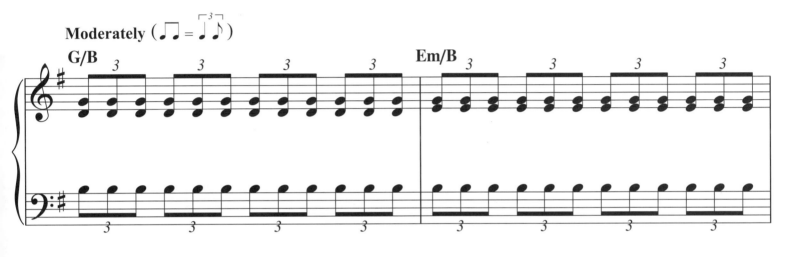

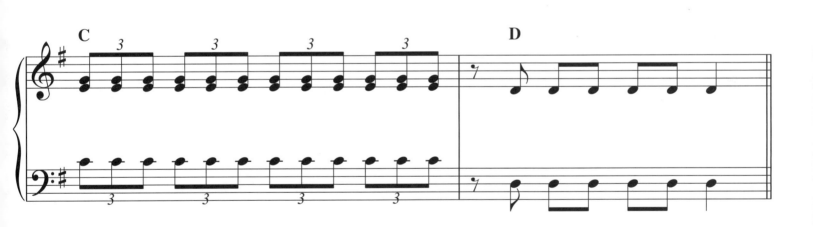

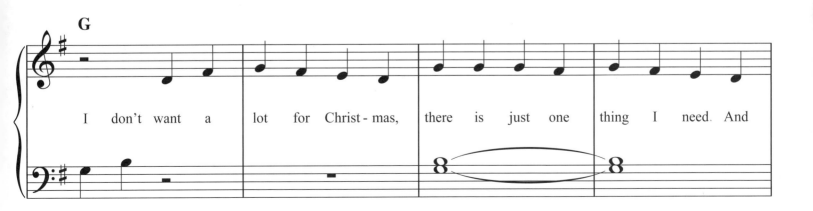

I don't want a lot for Christ-mas, there is just one thing I need. And

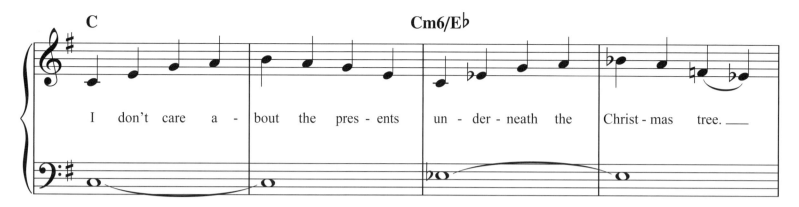

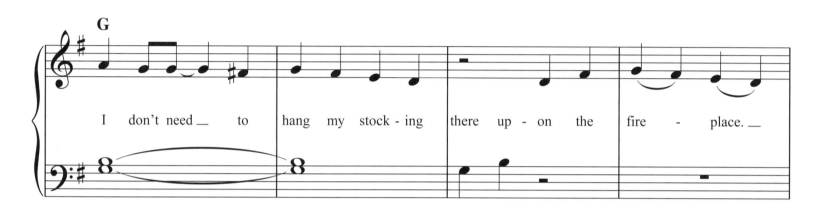

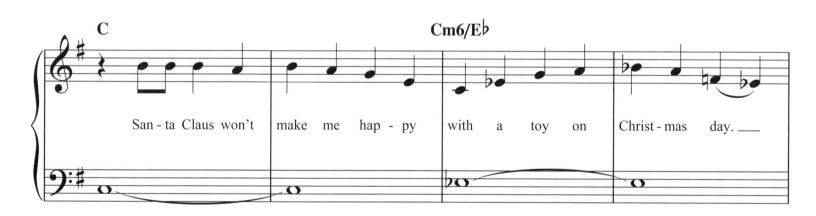

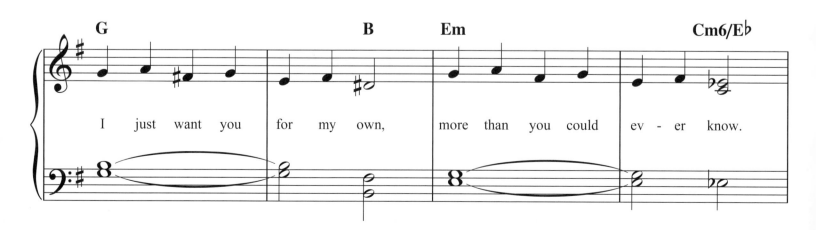

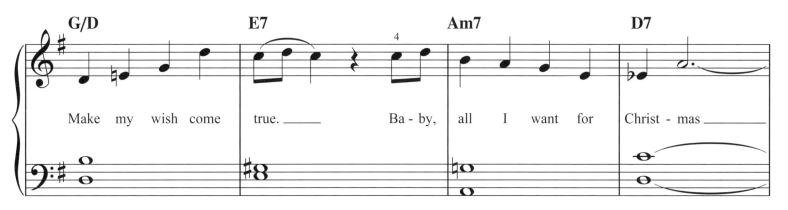

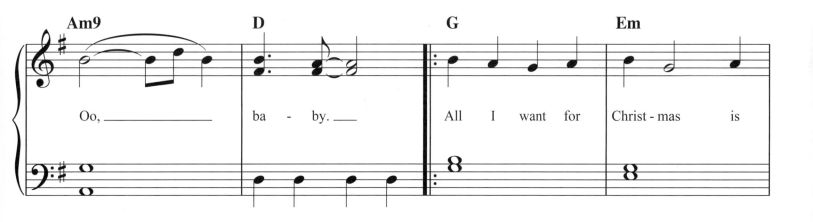

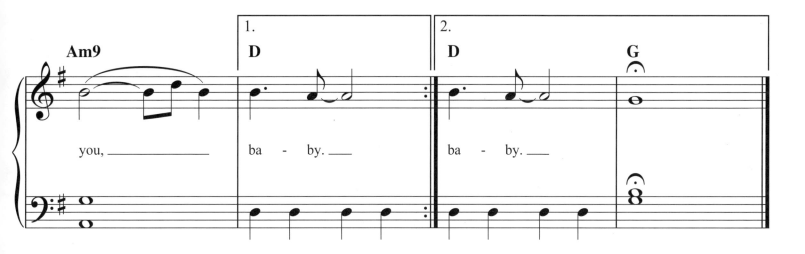

BLUE CHRISTMAS

Words and Music by BILLY HAYES
and JAY JOHNSON

Moderately, in 2

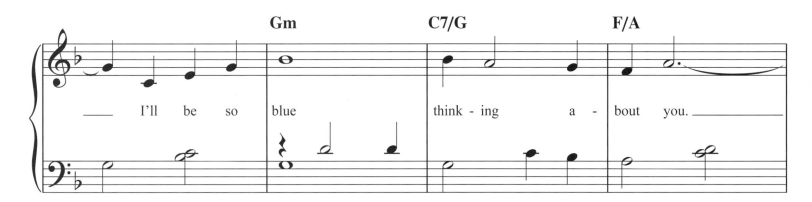

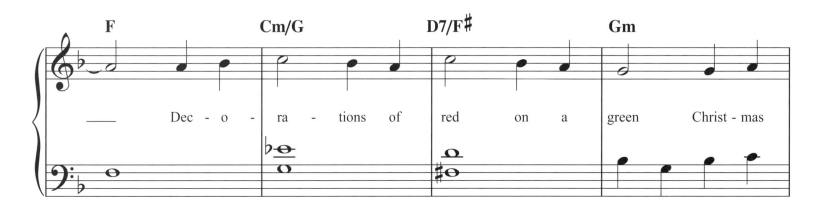

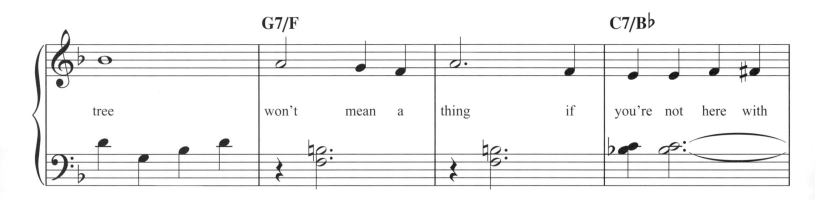

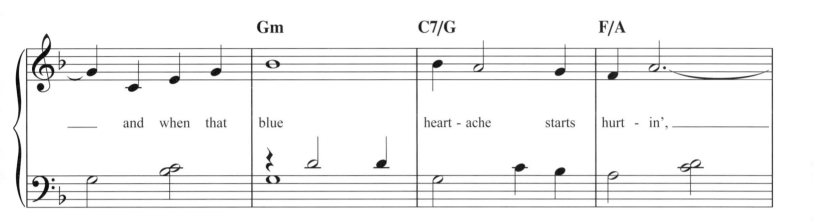

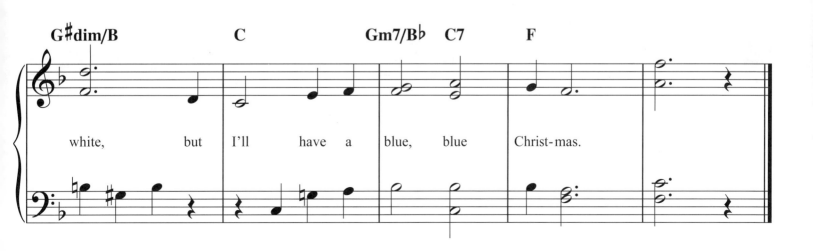

THE CHIPMUNK SONG

Words and Music by
ROSS BAGDASARIAN

Christ - mas, Christ - mas time is near,

time for toys and time for cheer.

We've been good but we can't last, hur - ry

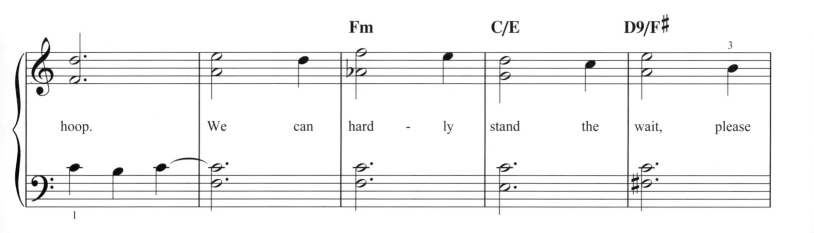

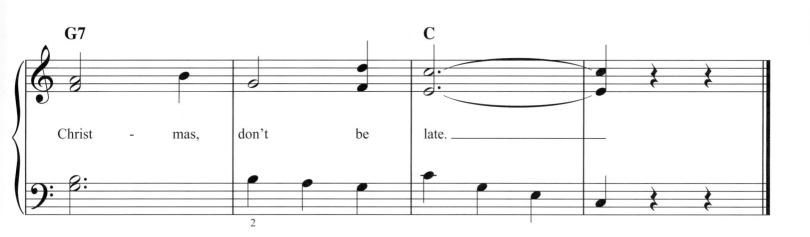

THE CHRISTMAS WALTZ

Words by SAMMY CAHN
Music by JULE STYNE

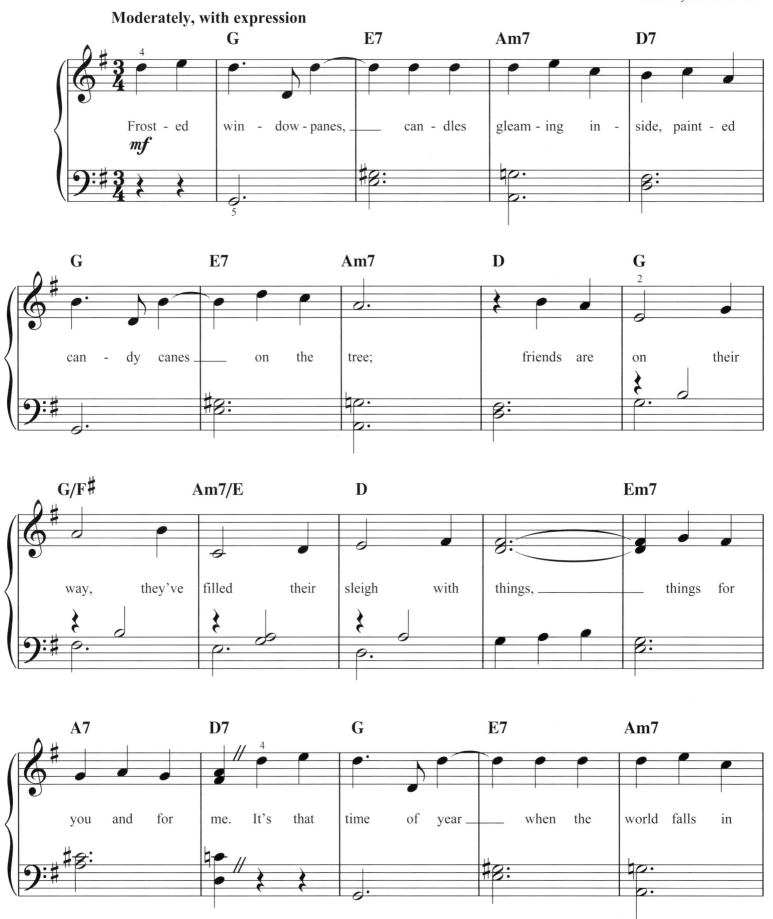

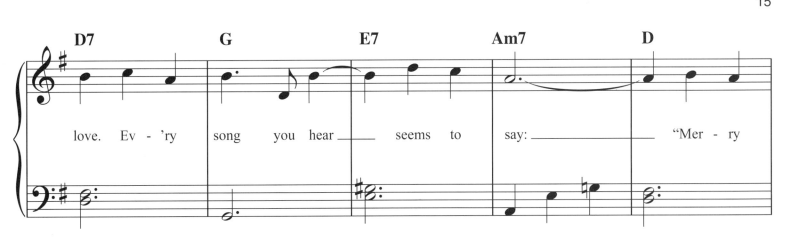

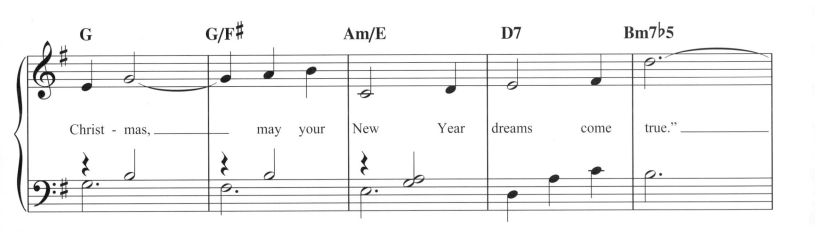

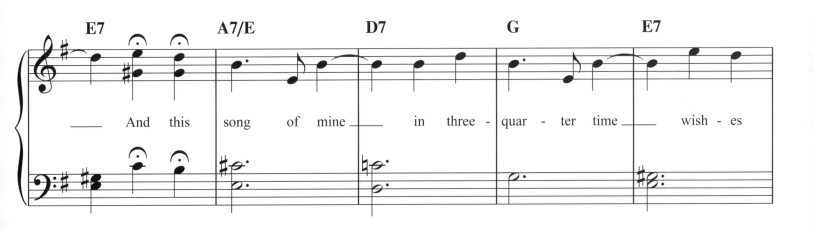

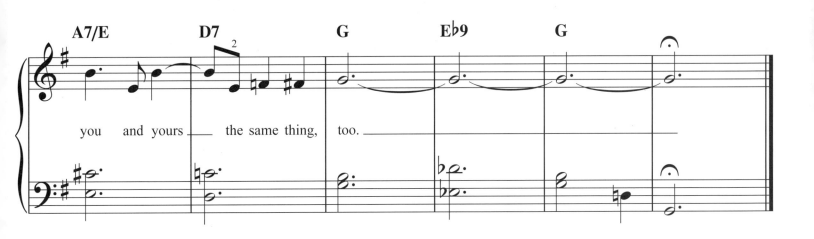

DO YOU HEAR WHAT I HEAR

Words and Music by NOEL REGNEY
and GLORIA SHAYNE

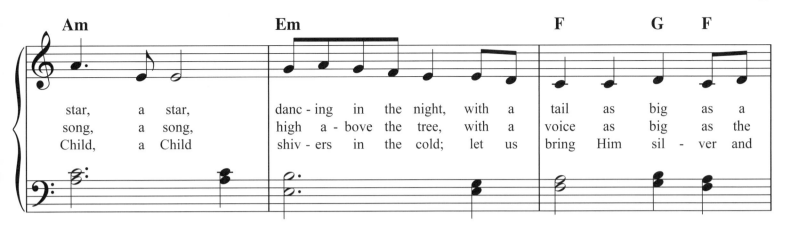

Am star, a star, / song, a song, / Child, a Child **Em** danc-ing in the night, with a / high a-bove the tree, with a / shiv-ers in the cold; let us **F** **G** **F** tail as big as a / voice as big as the / bring Him sil - ver and

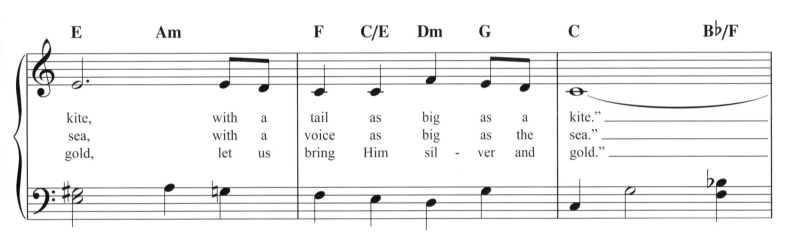

E **Am** kite, / sea, / gold, with a / with a / let us **F** **C/E** **Dm** **G** tail as big as a / voice as big as the / bring Him sil - ver and **C** **Bb/F** kite." / sea." / gold."

1., 2. **C** ___ / ___ Said the / Said the *3.* **C** ___ Said the **Bb/F** king to the peo - ple ev - 'ry

C where, **G** **F** **G** "Lis - ten to what I say: **C** **G** **F** **G**

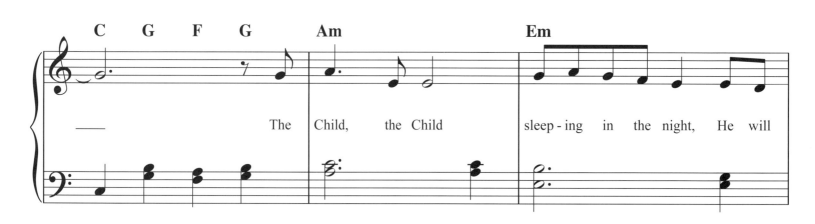

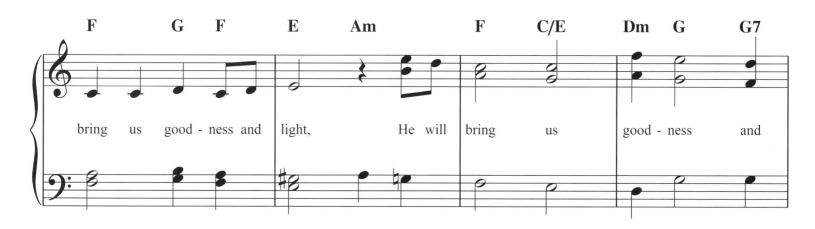

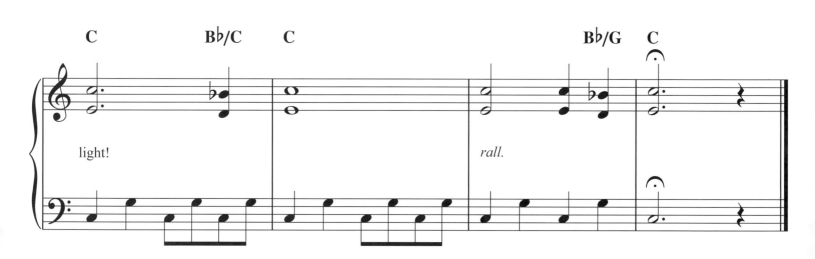

A HOLLY JOLLY CHRISTMAS

Music and Lyrics by
JOHNNY MARKS

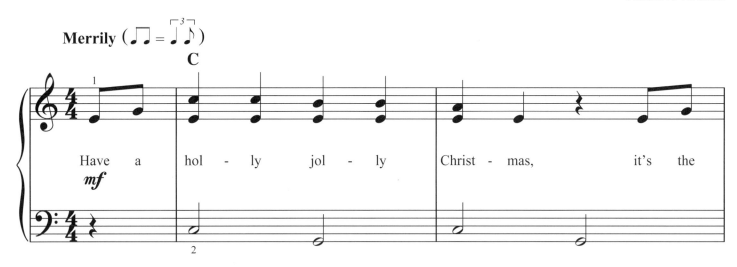

Have a   hol - ly   jol - ly   Christ - mas,   it's the

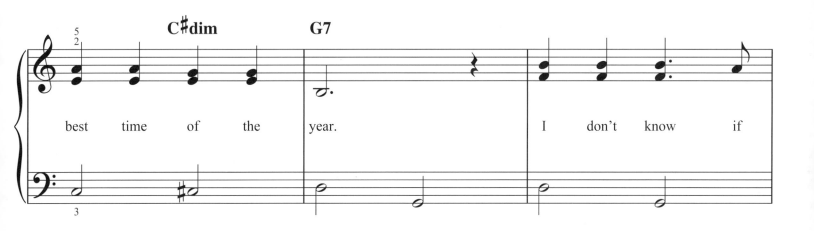

best time of   the   year.   I   don't know   if

there'll be snow, but let's all give a   cheer.   Have a

hol - ly jol - ly Christ - mas and when you walk down the

C♯dim

G7

street, say hel - lo to friends you know and

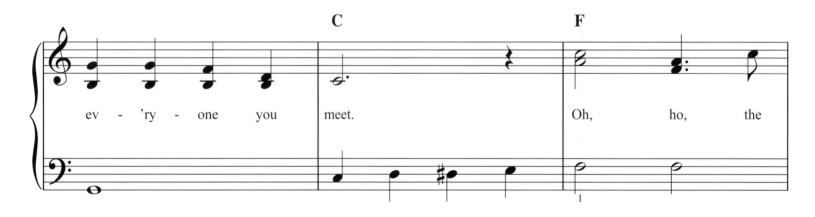

ev - 'ry - one you meet. Oh, ho, the

C **F**

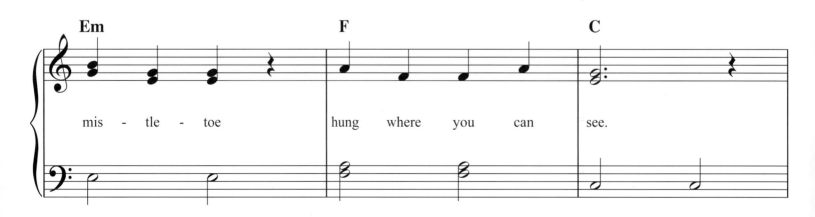

Em **F** **C**

mis - tle - toe hung where you can see.

Some - bod - y waits for you, kiss her once for

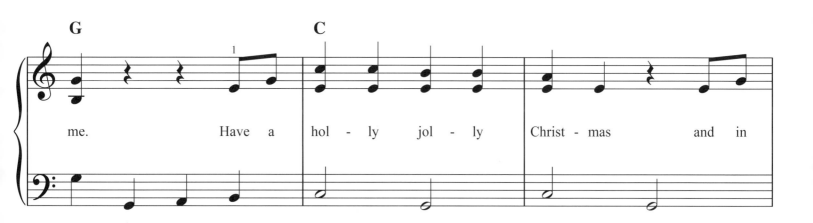

me. Have a hol - ly jol - ly Christ - mas and in

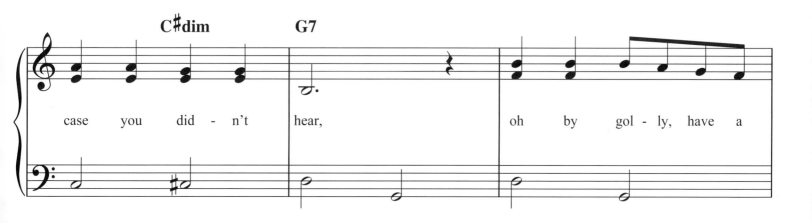

case you did - n't hear, oh by gol - ly, have a

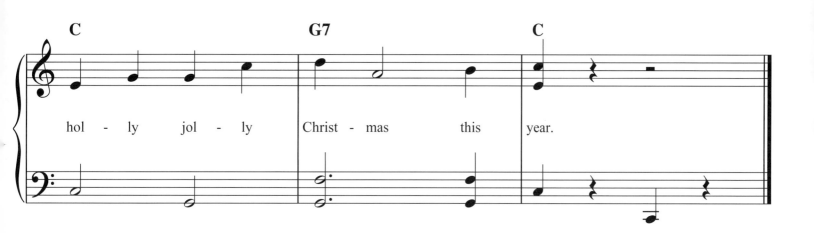

hol - ly jol - ly Christ - mas this year.

FELIZ NAVIDAD

Music and Lyrics by
JOSÉ FELICIANO

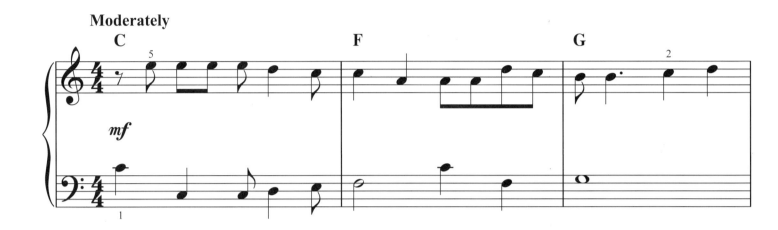

Fe - liz Na - vi - dad. _____

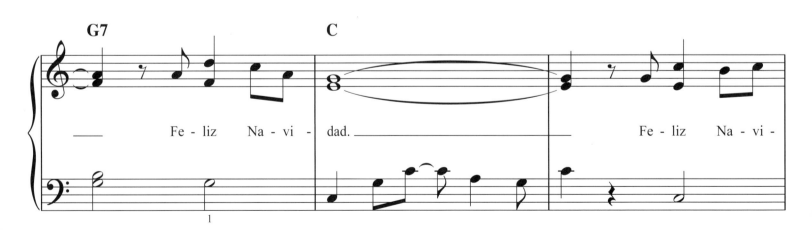

_____ Fe - liz Na - vi - dad. _____ Fe - liz Na - vi -

heart. _____

I want to wish you a Mer - ry Christ-mas

with mis - tle - toe and __ lots of cheer, _

with lots of laugh - ter through-

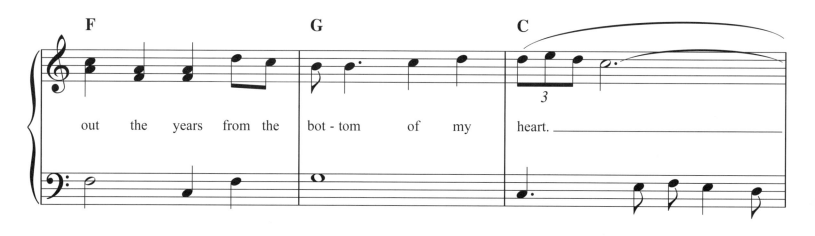

out the years from the bot - tom of my heart. _____

D.S. al Coda

__ Fe - liz Na - vi -

CODA

I HEARD THE BELLS ON CHRISTMAS DAY

Words by HENRY WADSWORTH LONGFELLOW
Adapted by JOHNNY MARKS
Music by JOHNNY MARKS

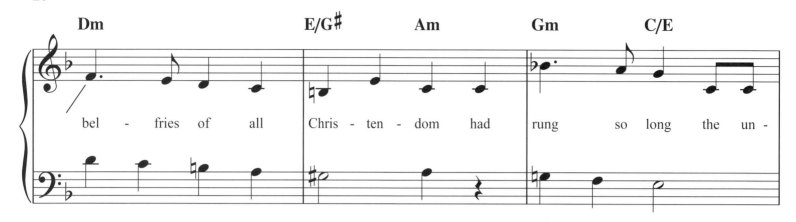

bel - fries of all | Chris - ten - dom had | rung so long the un -

Dm   *E/G♯*   *Am*   *Gm*   *C/E*

bro - ken song of | peace on earth good - | will to men.

Am   *D/F♯*   *Gm*   *C7*   *F/A*

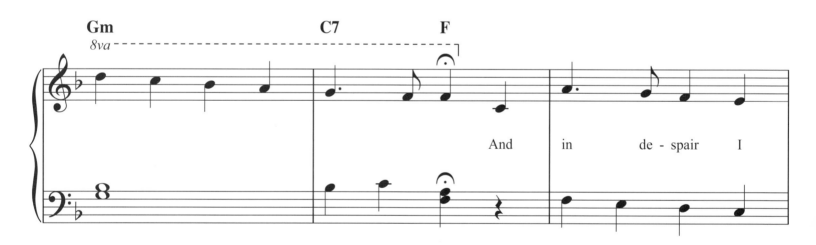

And | in de - spair I

Gm   *C7*   *F*

bowed my head. "There | is no peace on | earth," I said. "For

B♭   *C*   *Dm*   *E/G♯*   *Am*

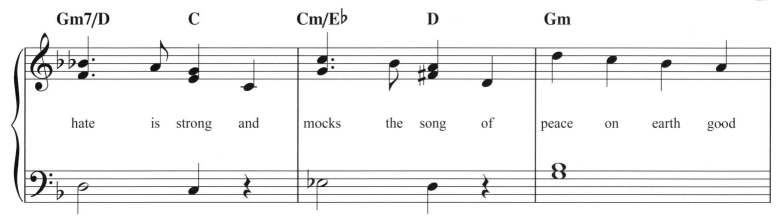

hate   is   strong   and   mocks   the   song   of   peace   on   earth   good

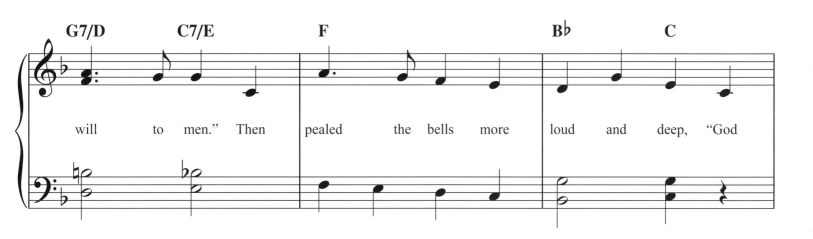

will   to   men."   Then   pealed   the   bells   more   loud   and   deep,   "God

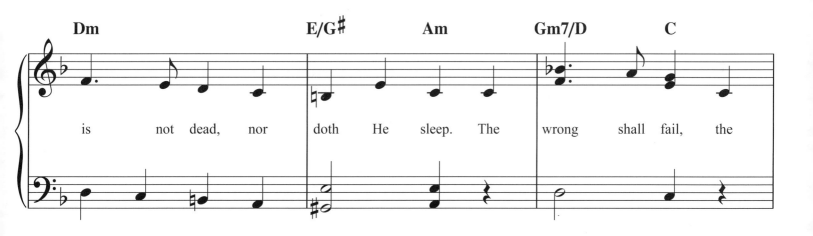

is   not   dead,   nor   doth   He   sleep.   The   wrong   shall   fail,   the

right   pre - vail   with   peace   on   earth,   good - will   to   men!"

rit.

HERE COMES SANTA CLAUS
(Right Down Santa Claus Lane)

Words and Music by GENE AUTRY
and OAKLEY HALDEMAN

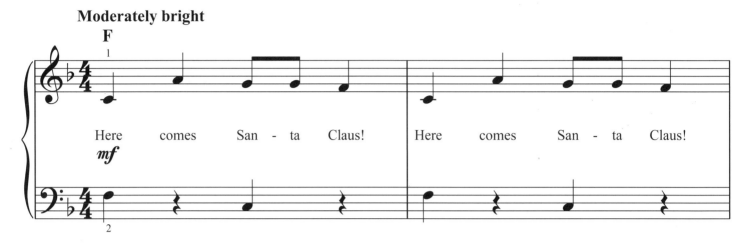

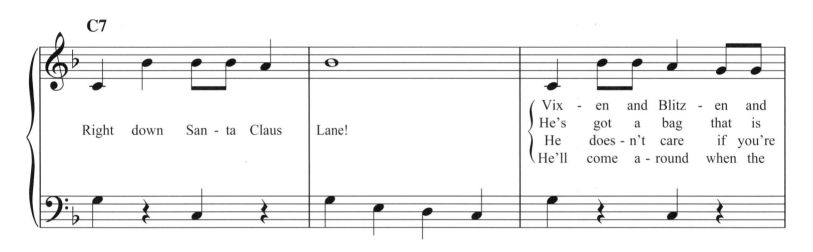

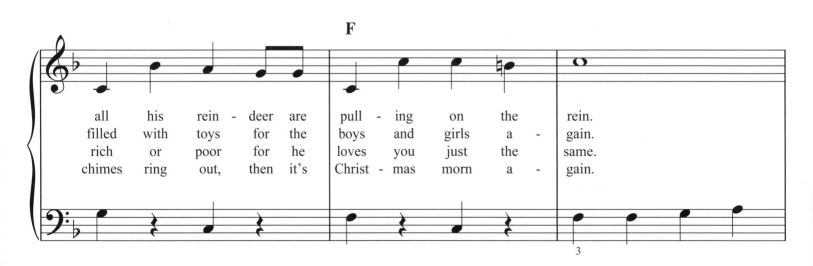

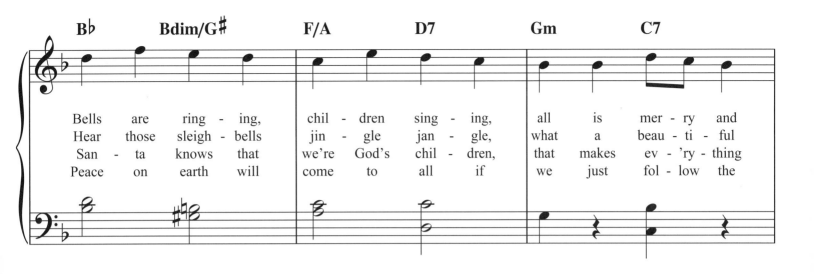

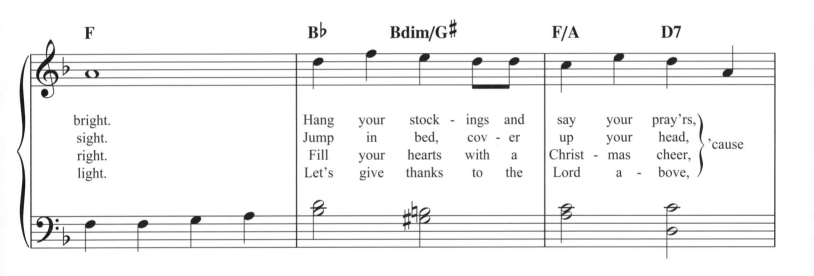

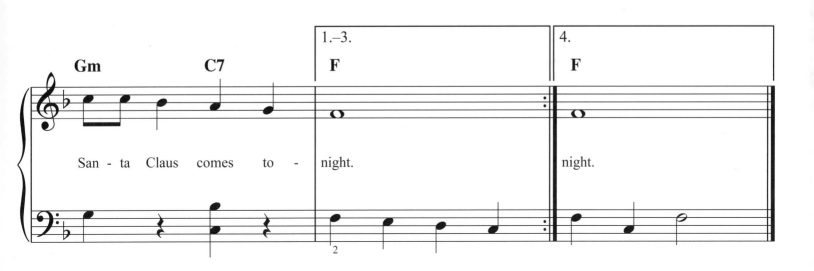

I WONDER AS I WANDER

By JOHN JACOB NILES

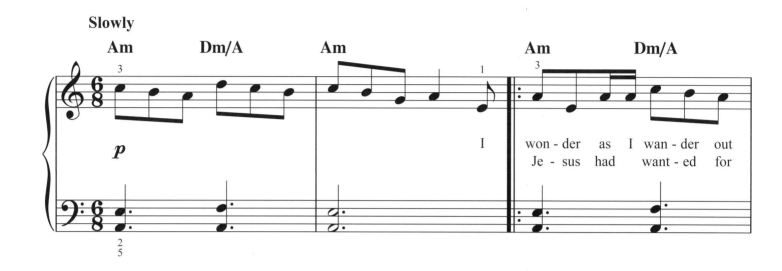

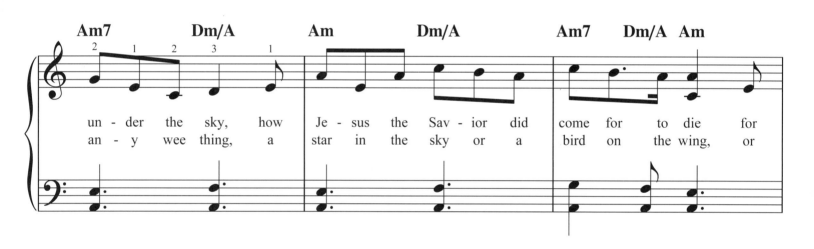

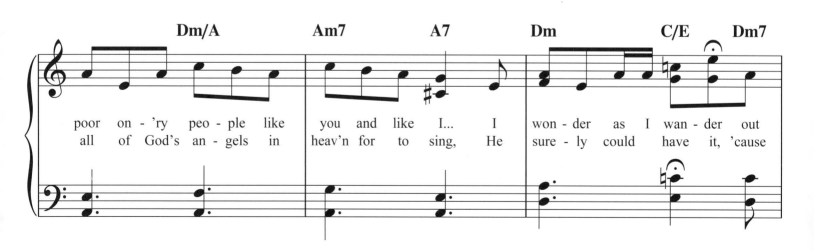

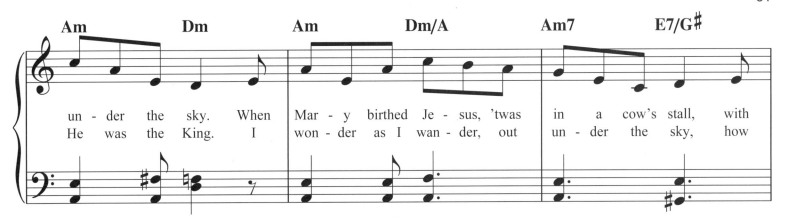

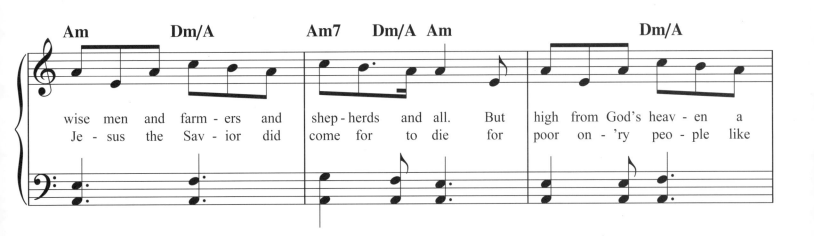

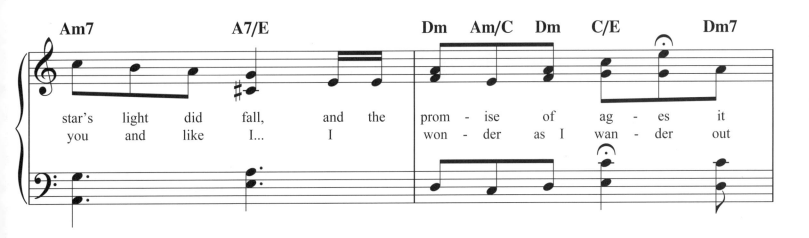

IT'S BEGINNING TO LOOK LIKE CHRISTMAS

By MEREDITH WILLSON

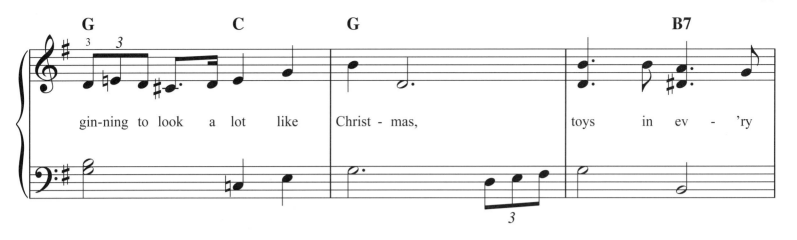

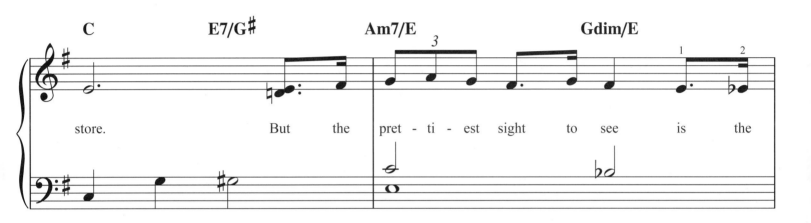

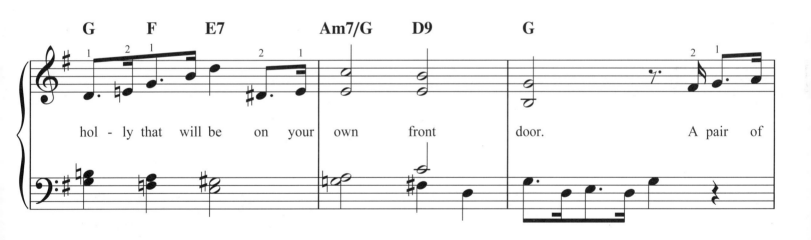

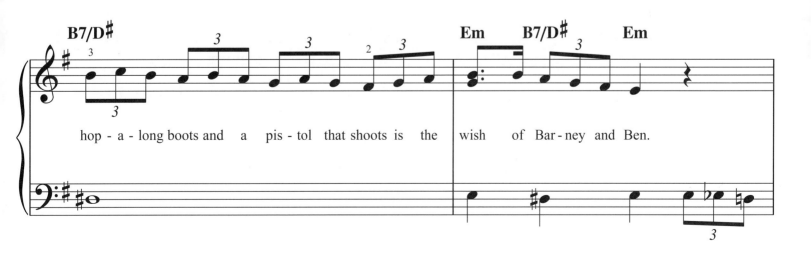

Dolls that will talk and will go for a walk is the hope of Jan - ice and Jen. And

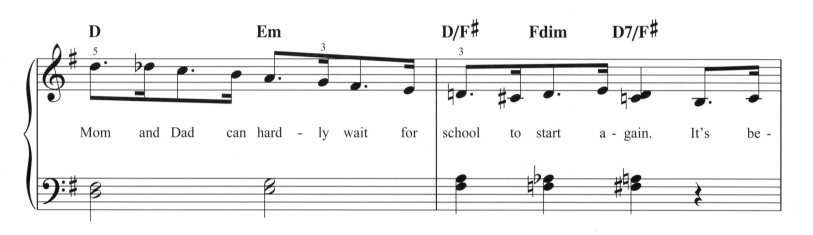

Mom and Dad can hard - ly wait for school to start a - gain. It's be -

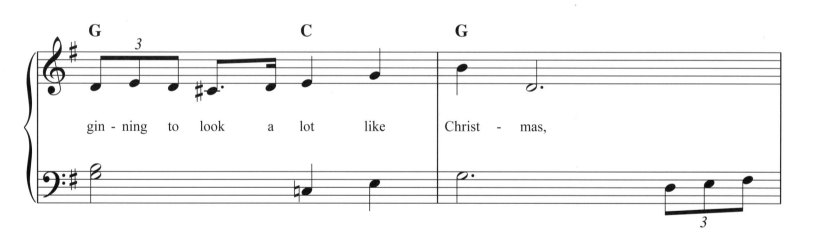

gin - ning to look a lot like Christ - mas,

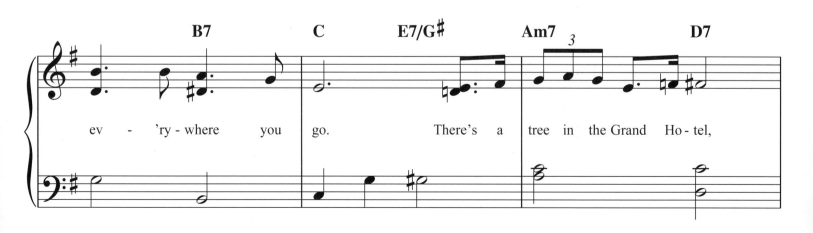

ev - 'ry - where you go. There's a tree in the Grand Ho - tel,

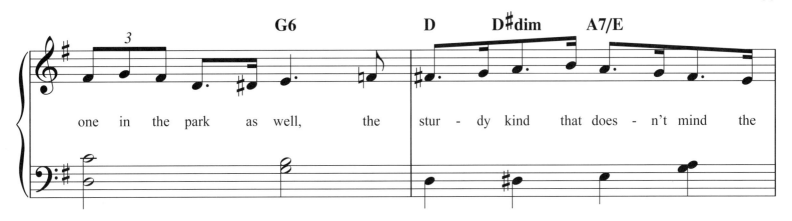

one in the park as well, the stur-dy kind that does-n't mind the

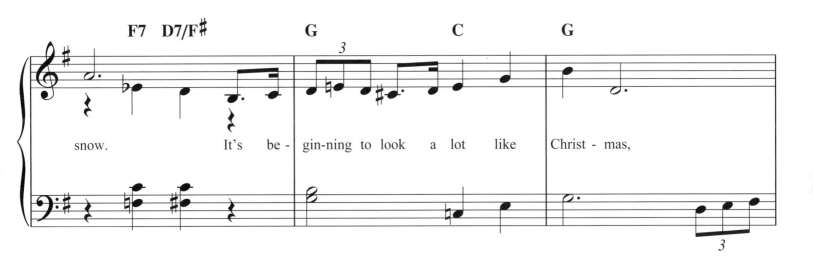

snow. It's be- gin-ning to look a lot like Christ - mas,

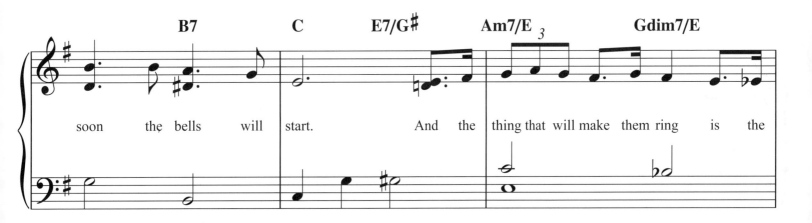

soon the bells will start. And the thing that will make them ring is the

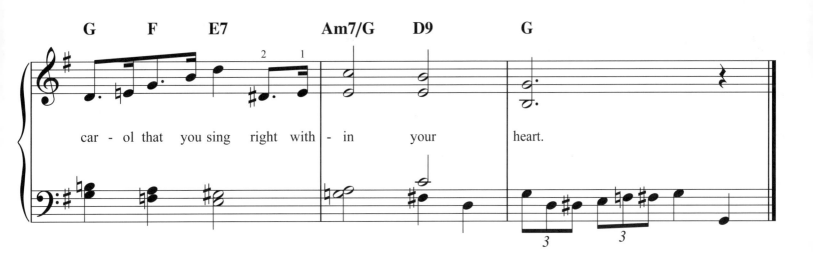

car - ol that you sing right with - in your heart.

LET IT SNOW! LET IT SNOW! LET IT SNOW!

Words by SAMMY CAHN
Music by JULE STYNE

hate go-ing out in the storm; but if you'll real-ly hold me tight,

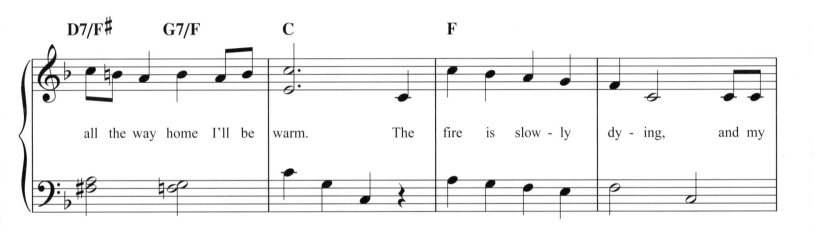

all the way home I'll be warm. The fire is slow-ly dy - ing, and my

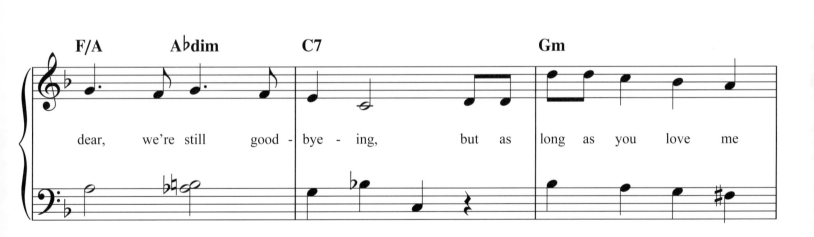

dear, we're still good - bye - ing, but as long as you love me

so, let it snow, let it snow, let it snow.

LITTLE SAINT NICK

Words and Music by BRIAN WILSON
and MIKE LOVE

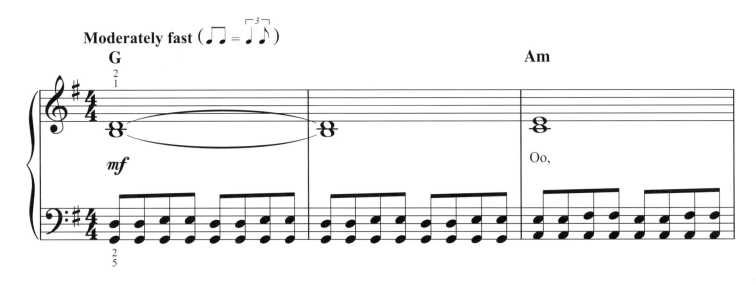

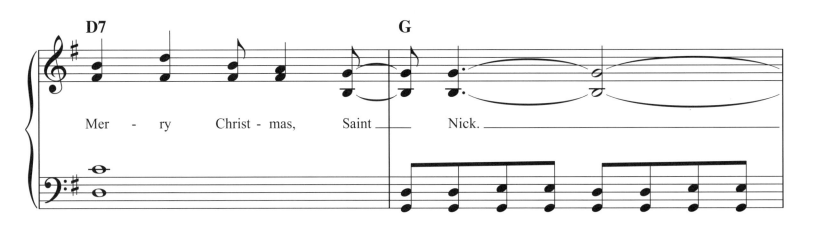

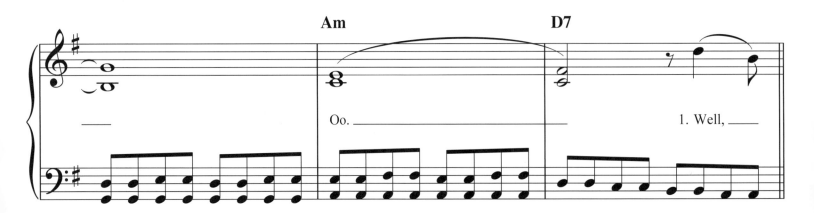

39

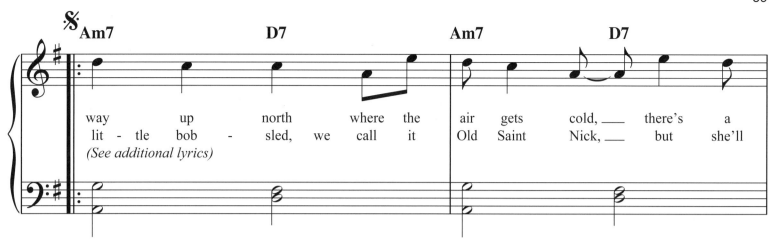

way up north where the air gets cold, ___ there's a
lit - tle bob - sled, we call it Old Saint Nick, ___ but she'll
(See additional lyrics)

tale a - bout Christ - mas that you've all been told. ___ And a
walk a to - bog - gan with a four - speed stick. ___ She's

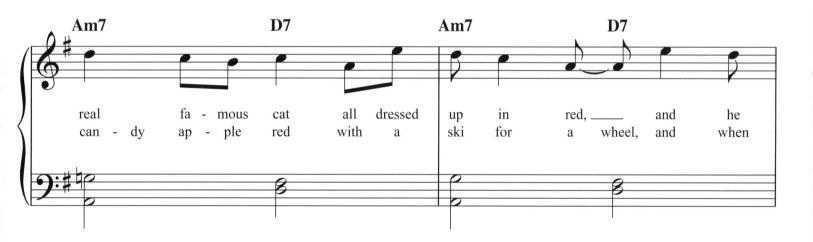

real fa - mous cat all dressed up in red, ___ and he
can - dy ap - ple red with a ski for a wheel, and when

spends the whole ___ year work - in' out on his sled. ___ } It's the Lit - tle Saint Nick. (Lit - tle
San - ta hits the gas, man, just watch her ___ peel. ___ }

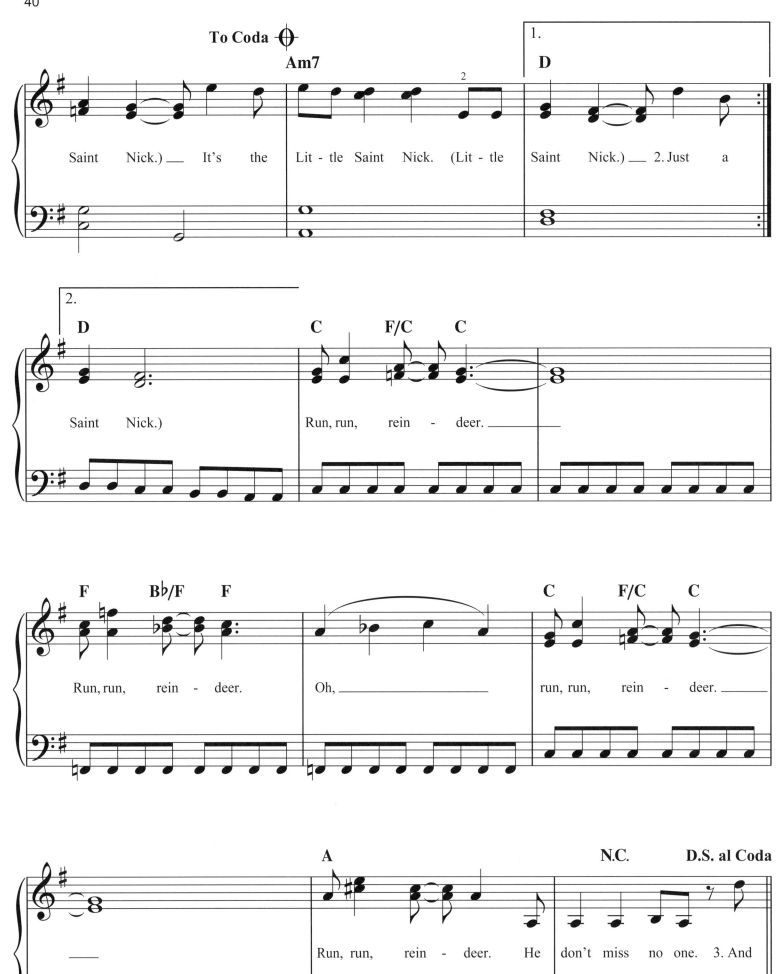

CODA

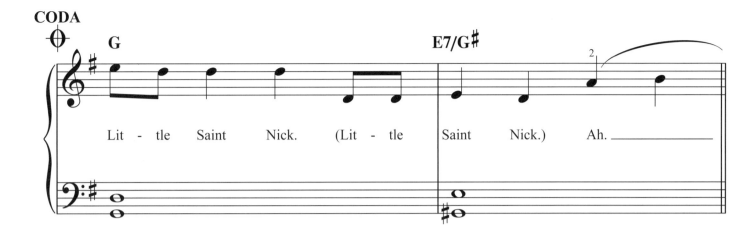

Lit - tle Saint Nick. (Lit - tle Saint Nick.) Ah. ____

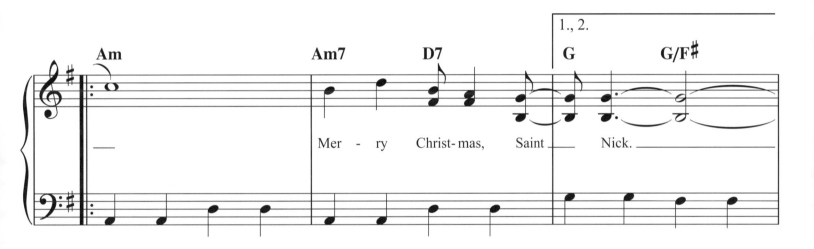

____ Mer - ry Christ- mas, Saint ____ Nick.

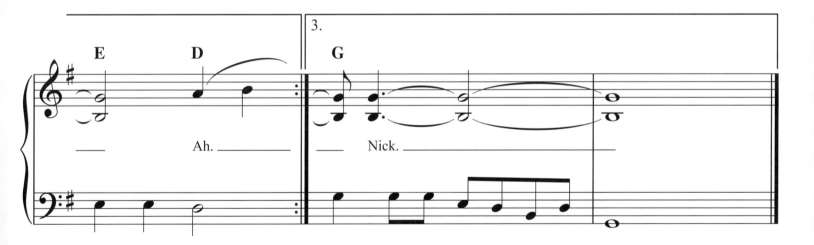

Ah. ____ Nick. ____

Additional Lyrics

3. And haulin' through the snow at a fright'nin' speed,
   With half a dozen deer with Rudy to lead,
   He's gotta wear his goggles 'cause the snow really flies,
   And he's cruisin' ev'ry pad with a little surprise.

A MARSHMALLOW WORLD

Words by CARL SIGMAN
Music by PETER DE ROSE

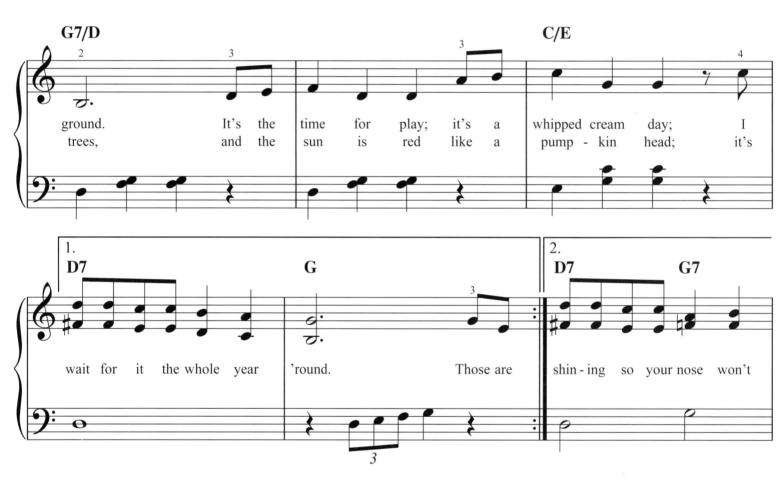

ev - er it snows. The world is your snow - ball; just for a song, get out and roll it a -

long. It's a yum, yum - my world made for sweet - hearts; _____ take a

walk with your fa - vor - ite girl. It's a sug - ar date; what if

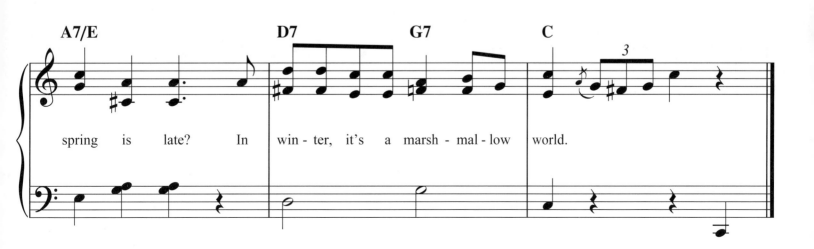

spring is late? In win - ter, it's a marsh - mal - low world.

MARY, DID YOU KNOW?

Words and Music by MARK LOWRY
and BUDDY GREENE

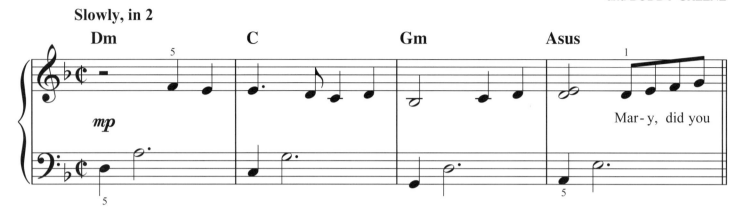

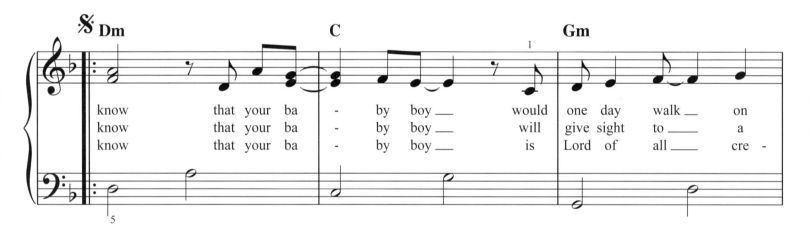

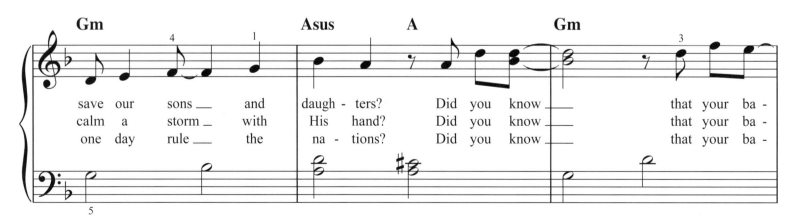

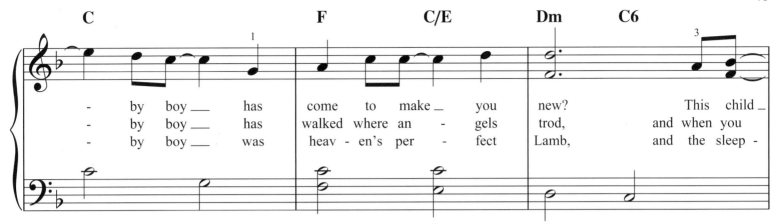

- by boy ___ has come to make ___ you new? This child ___
- by boy ___ has walked where an - gels trod, and when you
- by boy ___ was heav - en's per - fect Lamb, and the sleep -

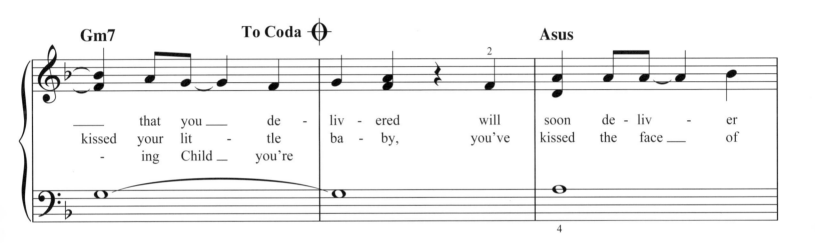

___ that you ___ de - liv - ered will soon de - liv - er
kissed your lit - tle ba - by, you've kissed the face ___ of
- ing Child ___ you're

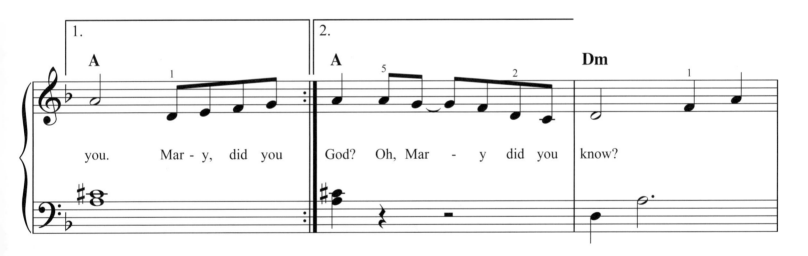

1.
you. Mar - y, did you

2.
God? Oh, Mar - y did you know?

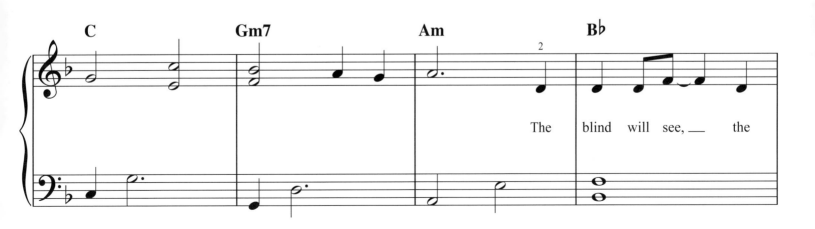

The blind will see, ___ the

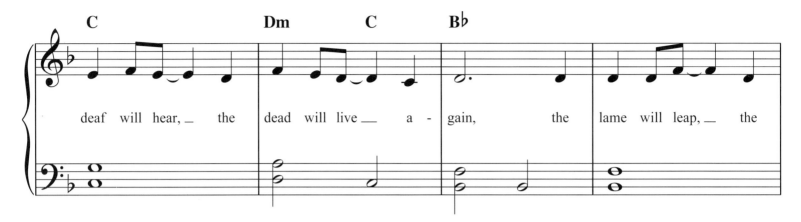

deaf will hear, __ the dead will live __ a - gain, the lame will leap, __ the

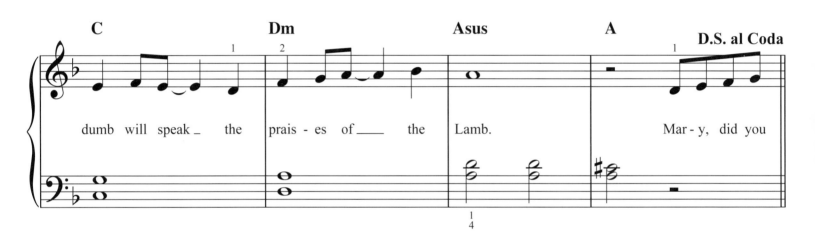

dumb will speak __ the prais - es of __ the Lamb. Mar - y, did you

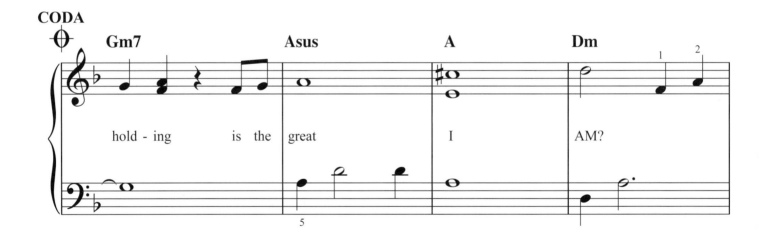

CODA

hold - ing is the great I AM?

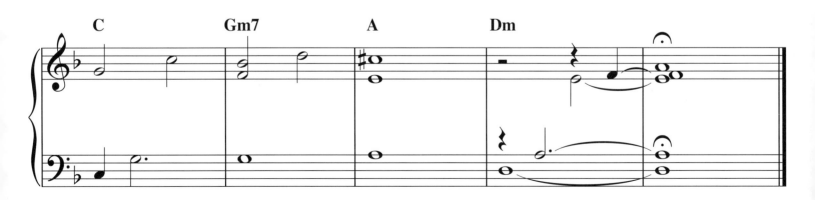

PRETTY PAPER

Words and Music by
WILLIE NELSON

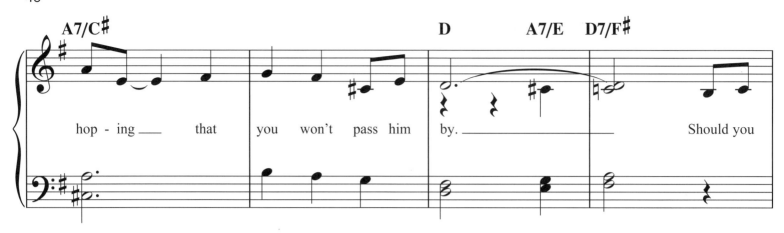

A7/C♯　　　　　　　　　　　　D　　　A7/E　D7/F♯

hop - ing ____ that　　you won't pass him　　by. _____ ____　　　　Should you

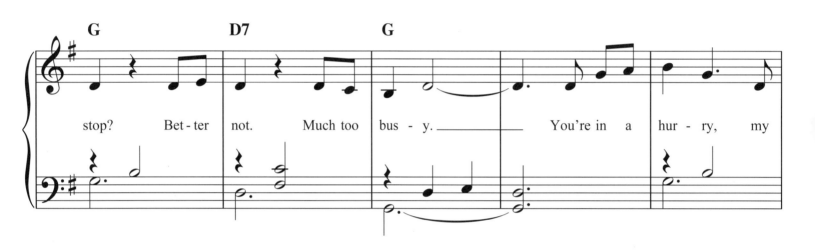

G　　　　　　　D7　　　　　　G

stop?　Bet - ter　not.　　Much too　bus - y. _____ ____　　You're in a　hur - ry,　my

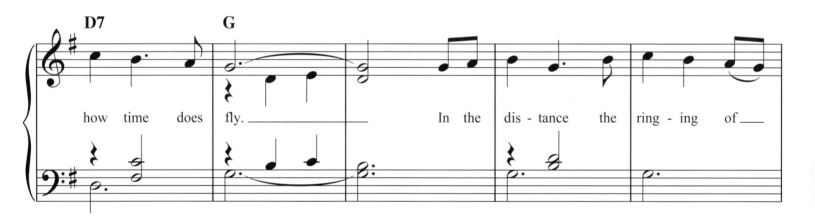

D7　　　　　　G

how time does　fly. _____ ____　　　　In the　dis - tance　the　ring - ing of ____

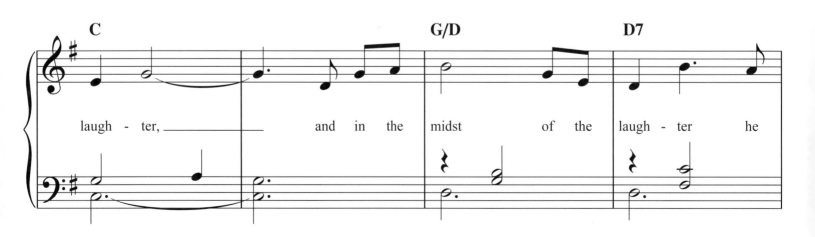

C　　　　　　　　　　　　　　　G/D　　　　　　D7

laugh - ter, _____ ____　　　　and in the　midst　　of the　laugh - ter　he

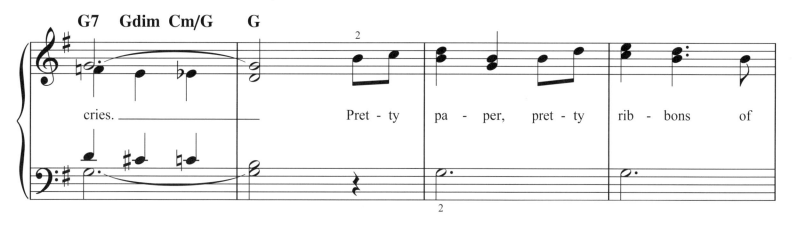

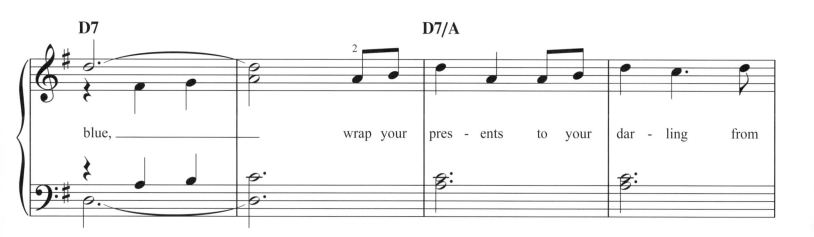

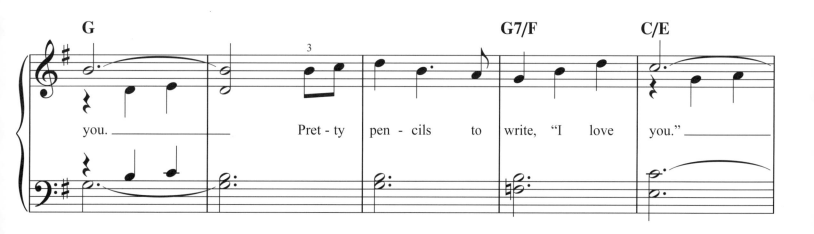

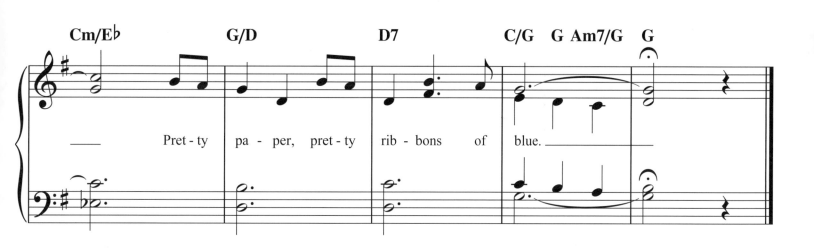

MISTLETOE AND HOLLY

Words and Music by FRANK SINATRA,
DOK STANFORD and HENRY W. SANICOLA

know.   Then   comes that   big night;   giv-ing the tree   the

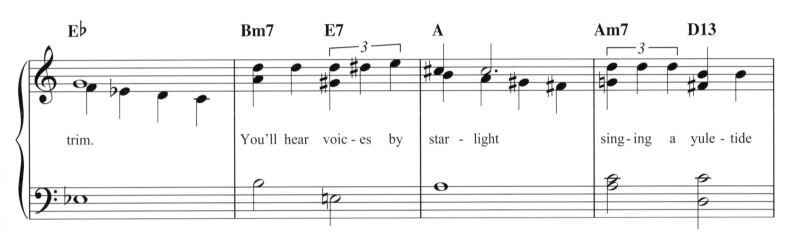

trim.   You'll hear voic-es   by   star - light   sing-ing a yule-tide

hymn.

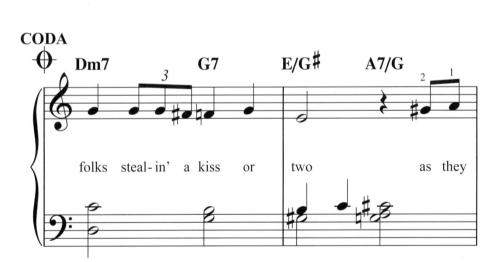

folks steal-in' a kiss   or   two   as they

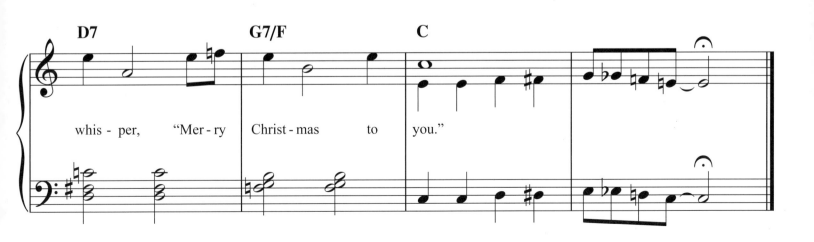

whis-per, "Mer-ry   Christ-mas   to   you."

THE MOST WONDERFUL TIME OF THE YEAR

Words and Music by EDDIE POLA
and GEORGE WYLE

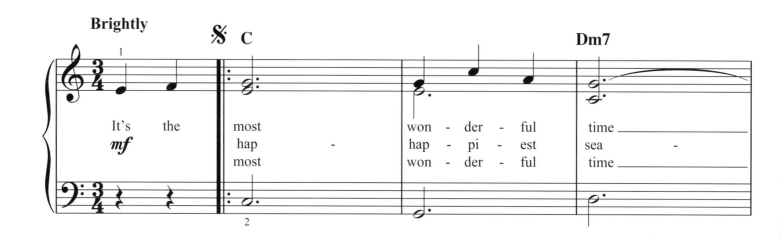

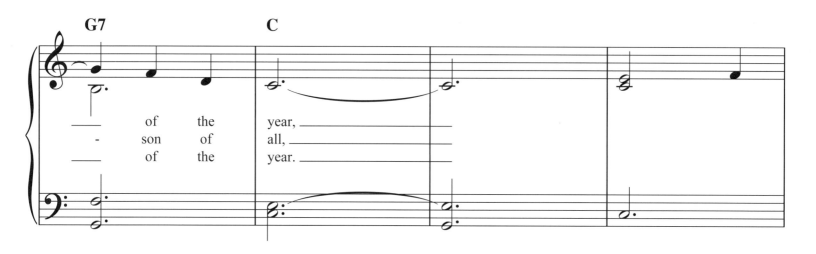

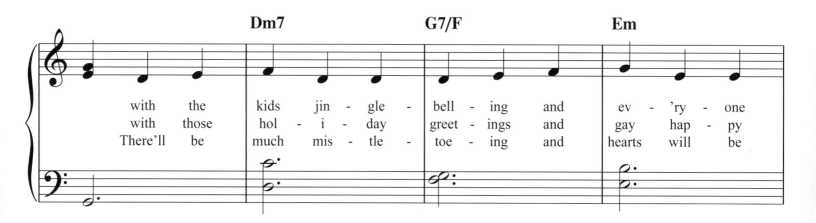

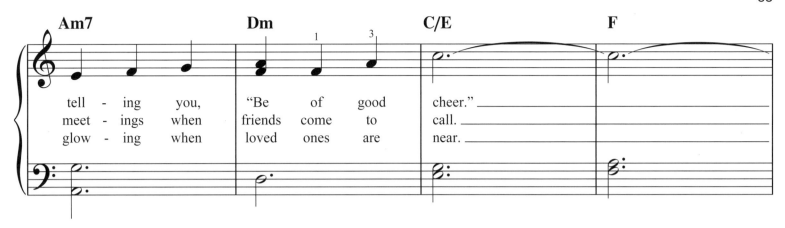

tell - ing you, "Be of good cheer."
meet - ings when friends come to call.
glow - ing when loved ones are near.

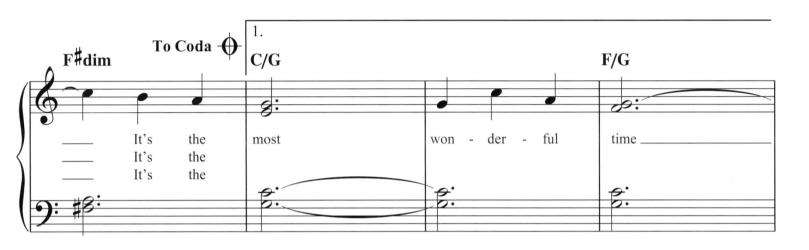

_____ It's the most won - der - ful time _____
_____ It's the
_____ It's the

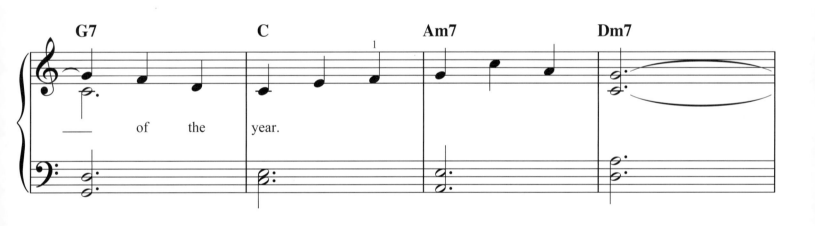

_____ of the year.

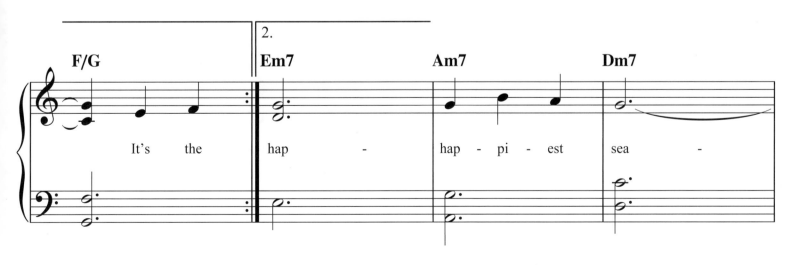

It's the hap - hap - pi - est sea -

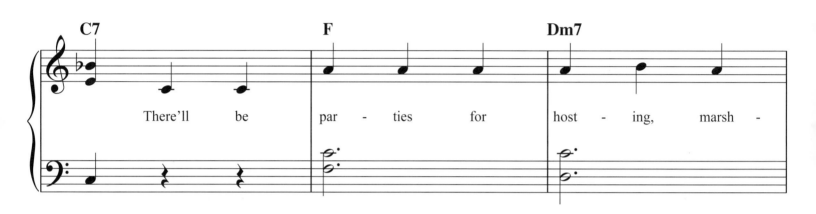

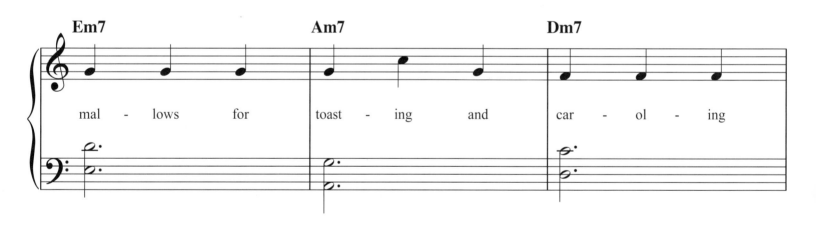

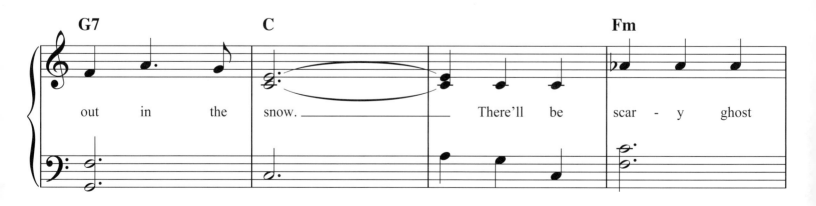

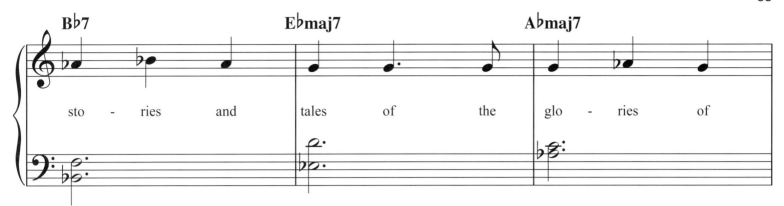

sto - ries and tales of the glo - ries of

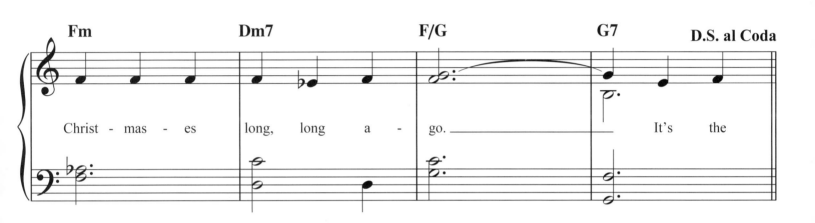

Christ - mas - es long, long a - go. It's the

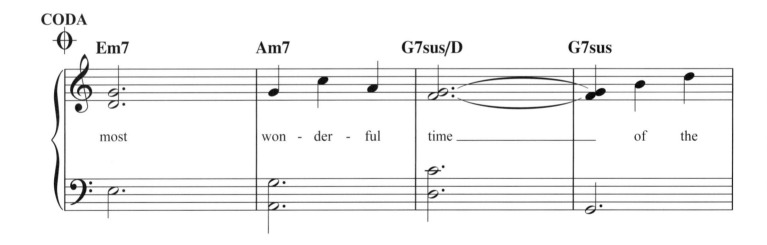

most won - der - ful time of the

year.

RUDOLPH THE RED-NOSED REINDEER

Music and Lyrics by
JOHNNY MARKS

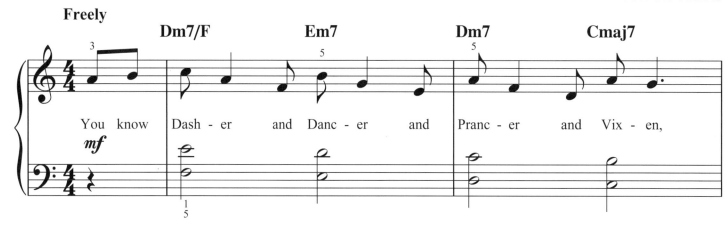

You know Dash-er and Danc-er and Pranc-er and Vix-en,

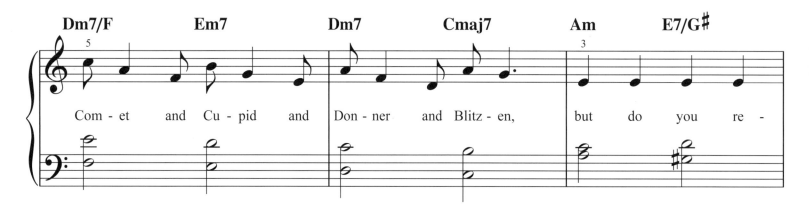

Com-et and Cu-pid and Don-ner and Blitz-en, but do you re-

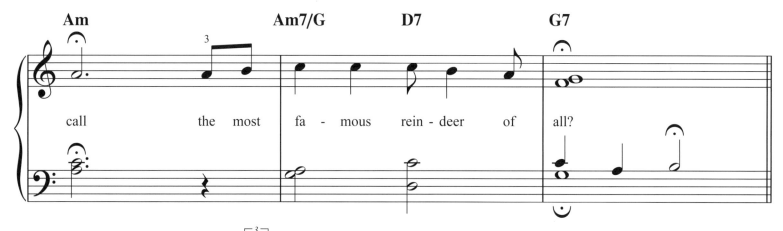

call the most fa-mous rein-deer of all?

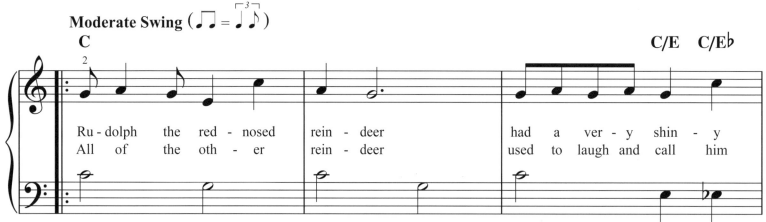

Ru-dolph the red-nosed rein-deer had a ver-y shin-y
All of the oth-er rein-deer used to laugh and call him

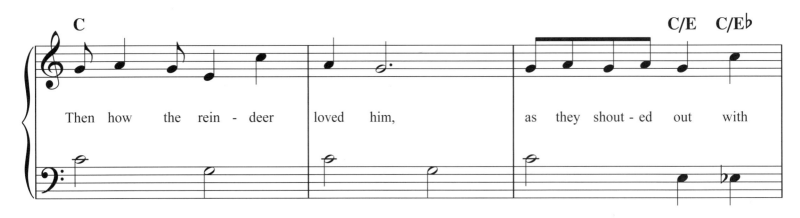

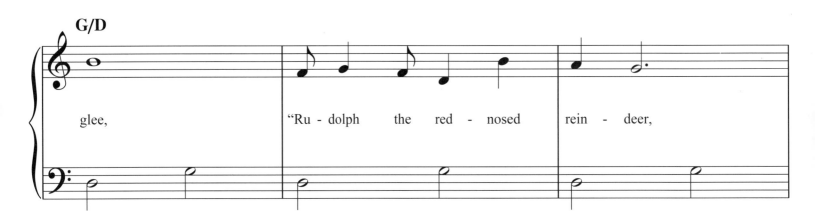

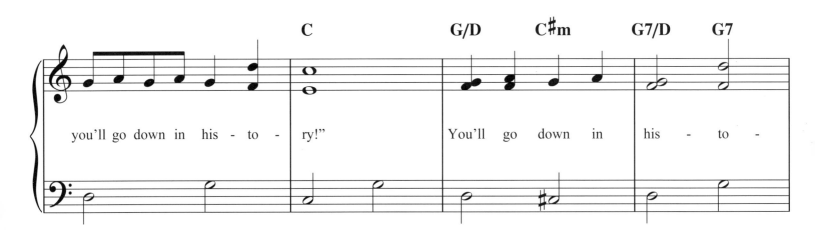

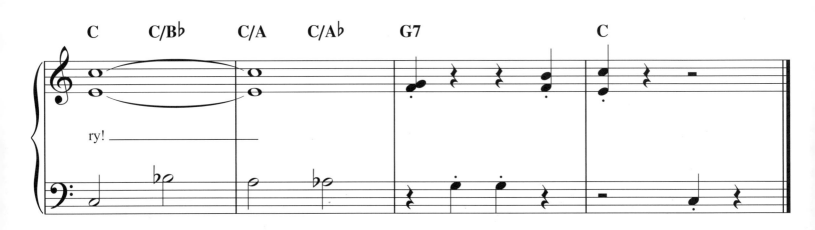

SANTA CLAUS IS COMIN' TO TOWN

Words by HAVEN GILLESPIE
Music by J. FRED COOTS

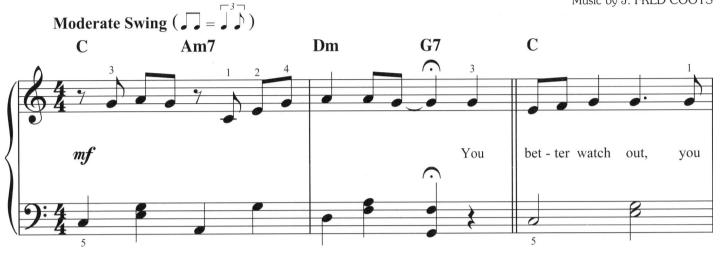

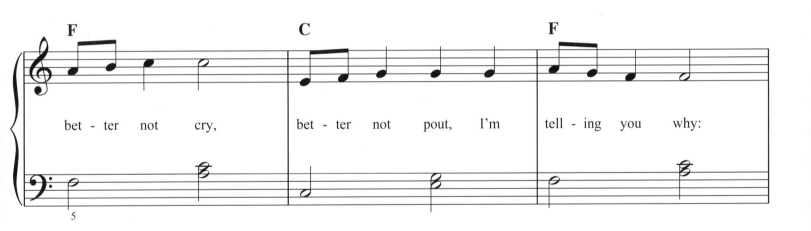

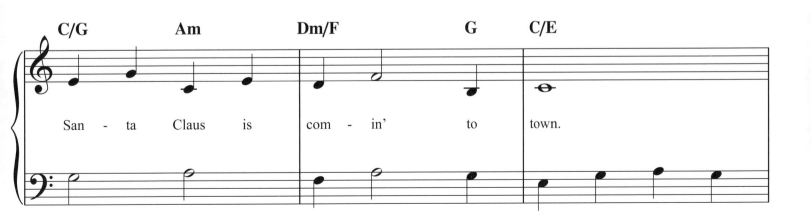

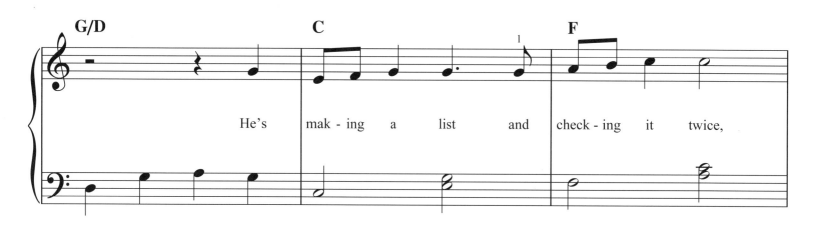

He's mak-ing a list and check-ing it twice,

gon-na find out who's naugh-ty and nice, San - ta Claus is

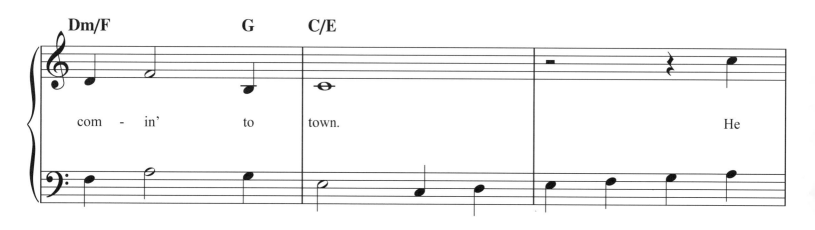

com - in' to town. He

sees you when you're sleep - in', he knows when you're a -

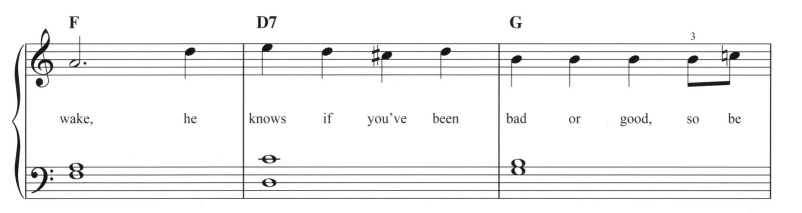

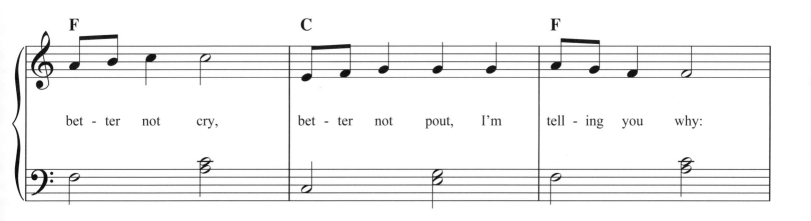

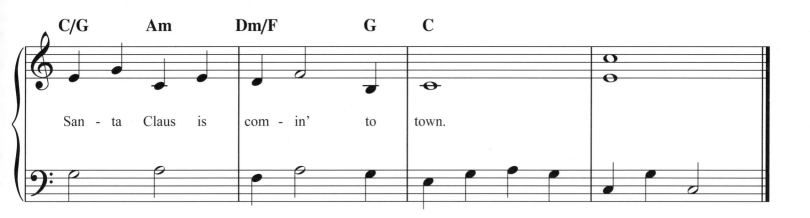

WE NEED A LITTLE CHRISTMAS

from MAME

Music and Lyric by
JERRY HERMAN

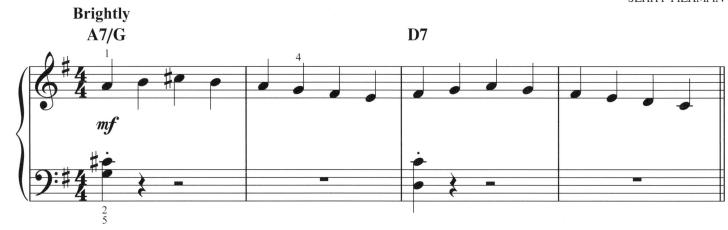

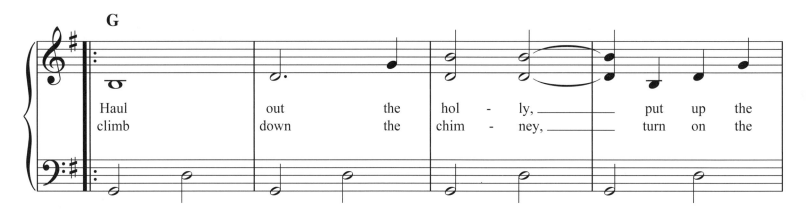

Haul out the hol- ly, _____ put up the
climb down the chim- ney, _____ turn on the

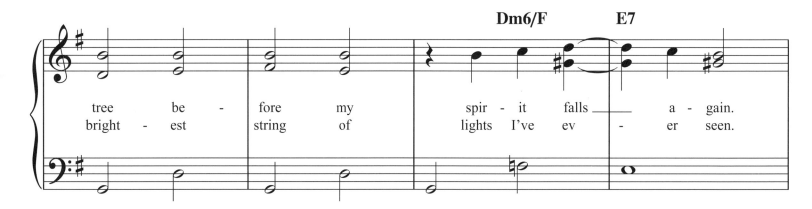

tree be - fore my spir - it falls _____ a - gain.
bright - est string of lights I've ev - er seen.

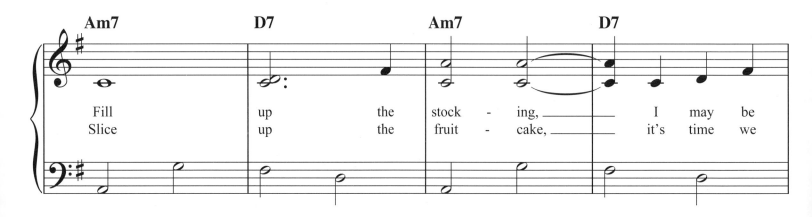

Fill up the stock - ing, _____ I may be
Slice up the fruit - cake, _____ it's time we

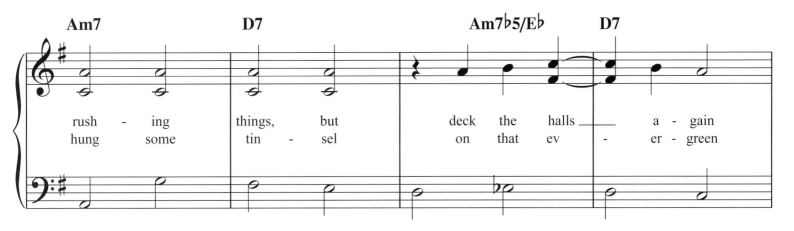

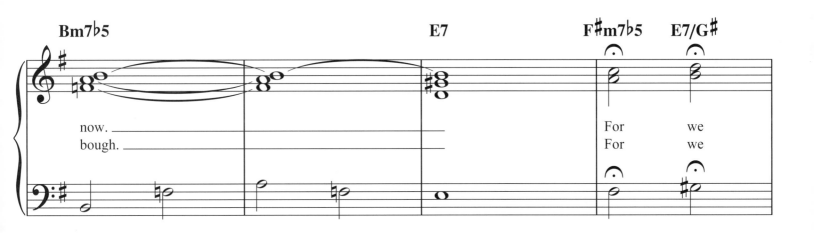

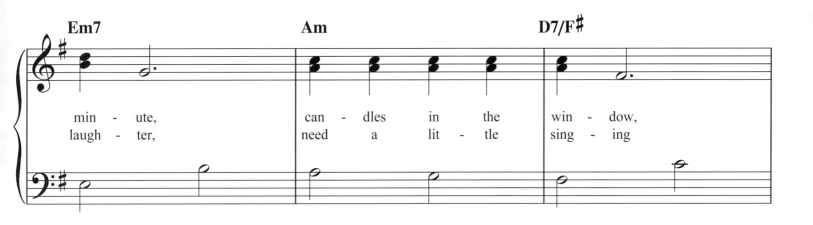

car - ols at the spin - et. Yes, we need a lit - tle
ring - ing through the raf - ter. And we need a lit - tle

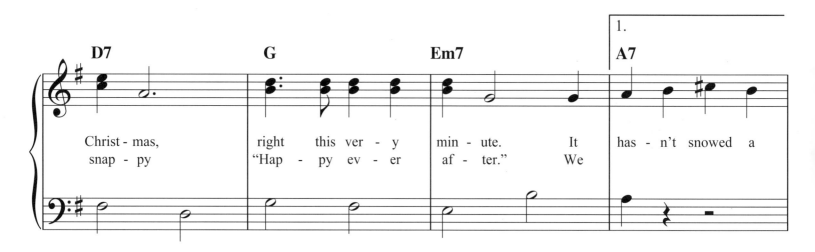

Christ - mas, right this ver - y min - ute. It has - n't snowed a
snap - py "Hap - py ev - er af - ter." We

sin - gle flur - ry, but San - ta, dear, we're in a hur - ry. So

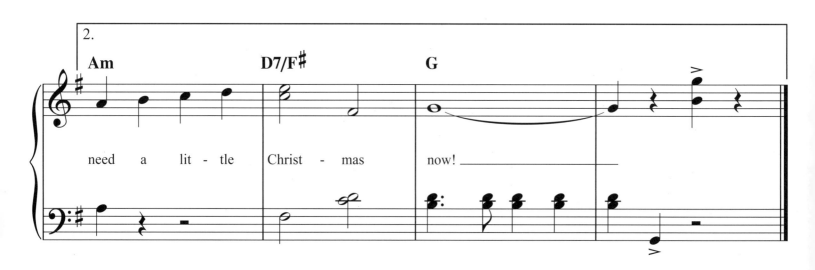

need a lit - tle Christ - mas now!

SILVER BELLS
from the Paramount Picture THE LEMON DROP KID

Words and Music by JAY LIVINGSTON
and RAY EVANS

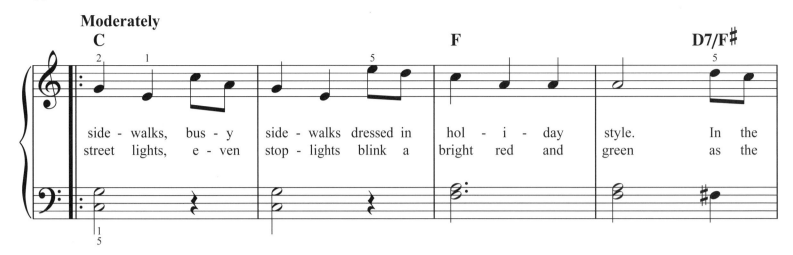

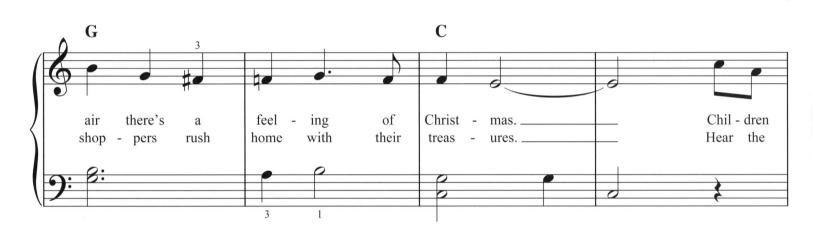

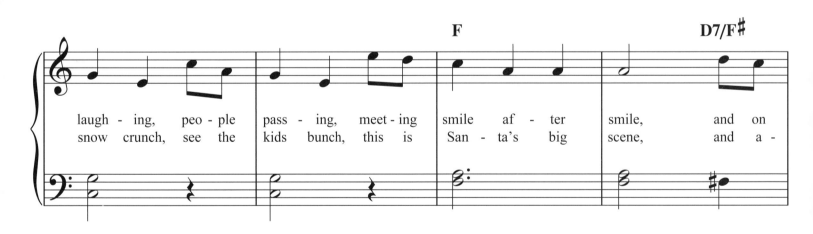

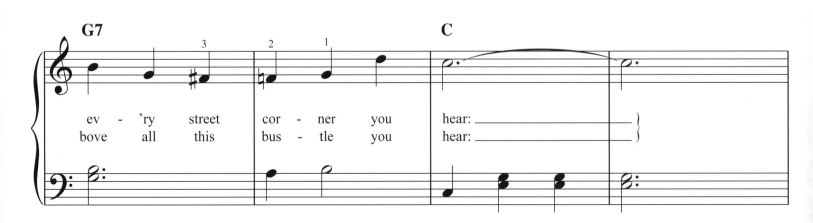

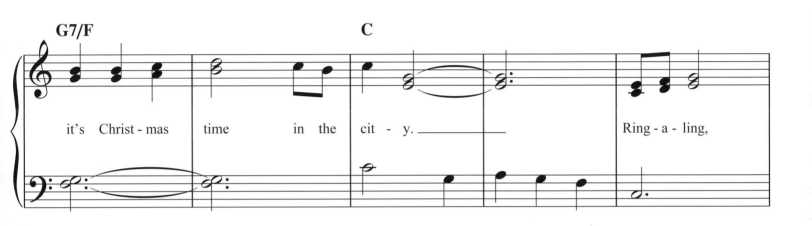

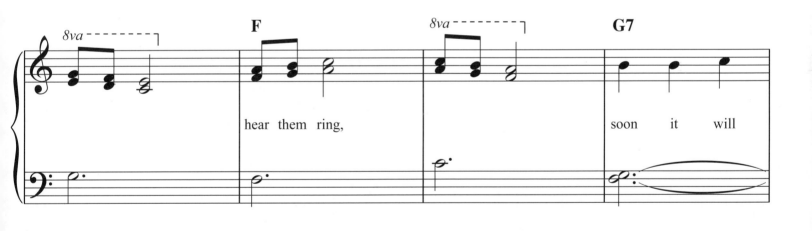

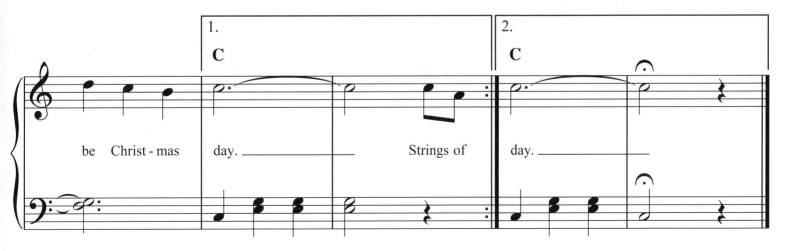

SOMEWHERE IN MY MEMORY

from the Twentieth Century Fox Motion Picture HOME ALONE

Words by LESLIE BRICUSSE
Music by JOHN WILLIAMS

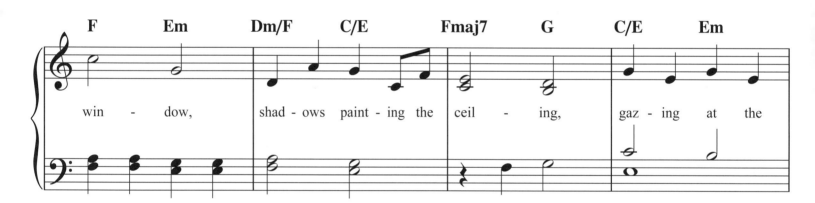

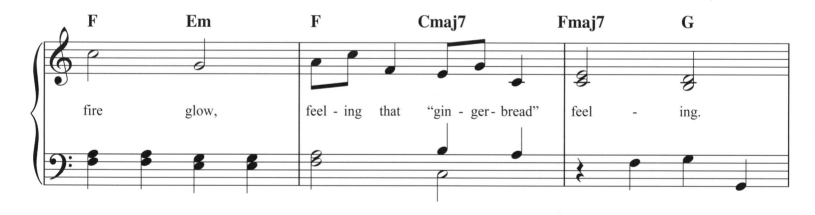

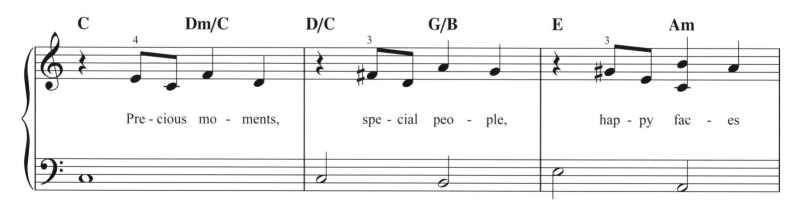

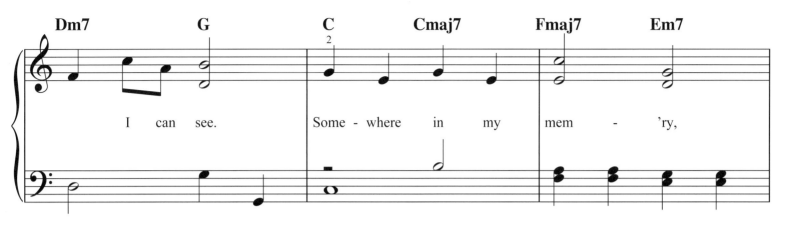

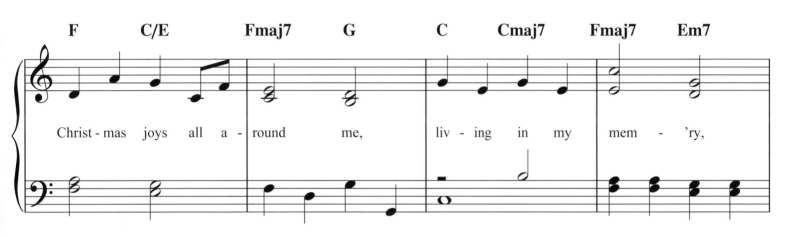

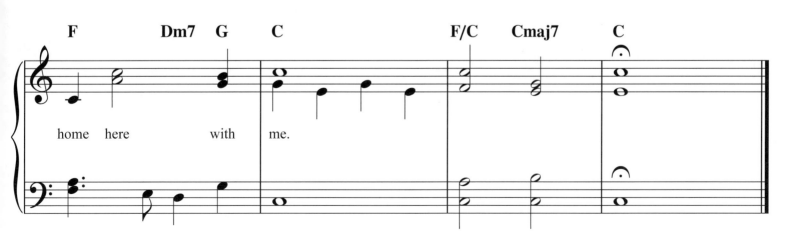

WHITE CHRISTMAS
from the Motion Picture Irving Berlin's HOLIDAY INN

Words and Music by
IRVING BERLIN

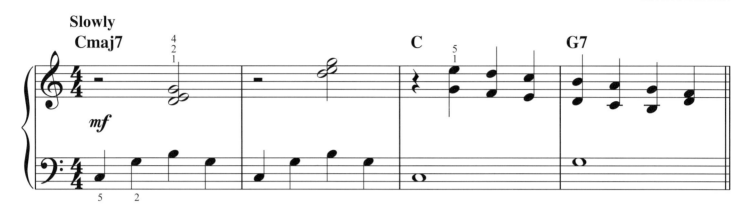

I'm dream - ing of a white

Christ - mas, just like the ones I used to

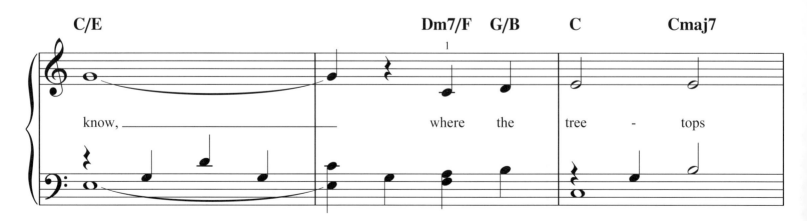

know, where the tree - tops

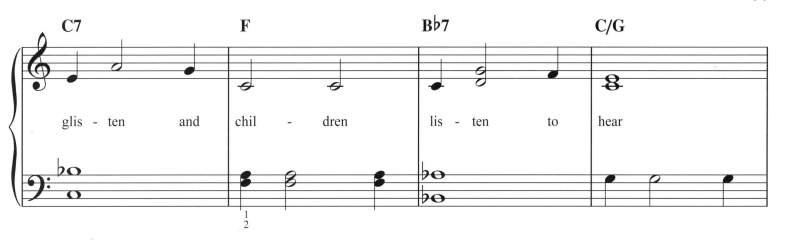

C7 · **F** · **Bb7** · **C/G**

glis - ten and chil - dren lis - ten to hear

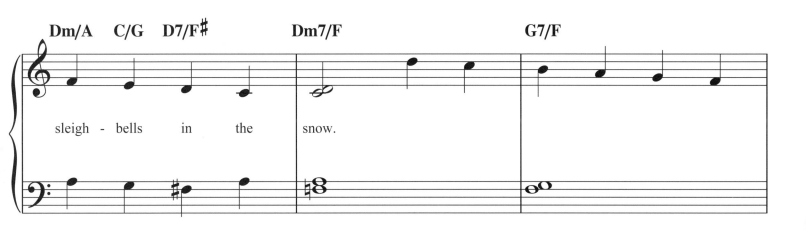

Dm/A **C/G** **D7/F#** · **Dm7/F** · **G7/F**

sleigh - bells in the snow.

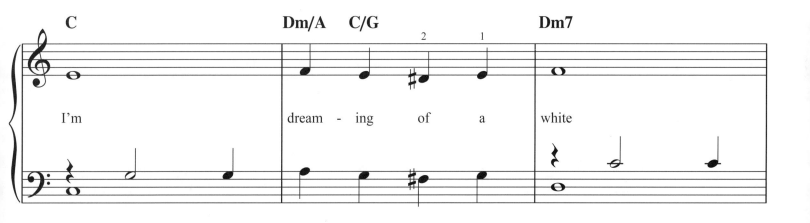

C · **Dm/A** **C/G** · **Dm7**

I'm dream - ing of a white

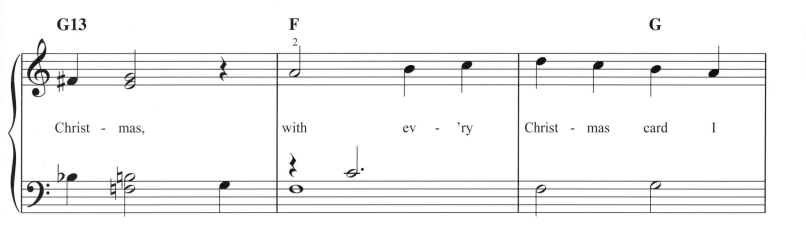

G13 · **F** · **G**

Christ - mas, with ev - 'ry Christ - mas card I

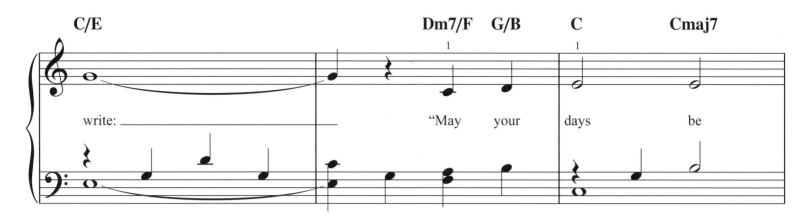

write: _____ "May your days be

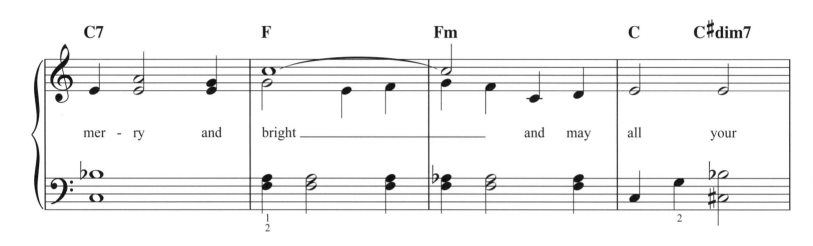

mer - ry and bright _____ and may all your

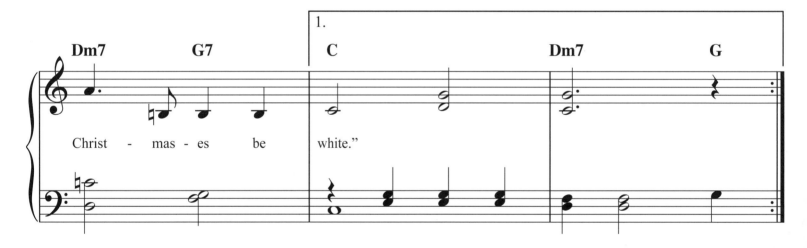

Christ - mas - es be white." white."

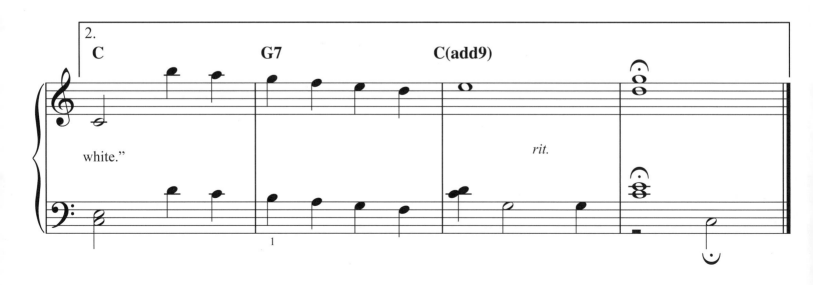

white."